Praise for
Rahab

"I'm always on the lookout for Shadia's newest Bible study. Each one is packed with rich insights, historical detail, and valuable life lessons. Shadia's expert scholarship combined with relevant personal experiences challenge me and help me grow deeper in my faith."

 —**Francine Rivers,** international best-selling author

"Insightful and rich in cultural details, Shadia Hrichi's new Bible study on Rahab takes the reader on a deep and meaningful journey. Because of it, I have a fresh understanding of the God who saves. Highly recommended."

 —**Robin Lee Hatcher,** Christy Award–winning author of *The Legacy of Faith* series and
  I'll Be Seeing You

"Pick up this study of Rahab and feel like you're sitting with a friend over coffee discussing what you're learning about the God who loves you. Over and over in this study, we see that Rahab's story is our story. It's the story of God pursuing his beloved people—us—with grace and persistence. With a much deeper dive into this woman in the lineage of Christ, Shadia challenges us to take our faith deeper with a relentlessly faithful God. She reminds us that no one, no matter who they are or what they've done, is outside of God's tender love. Just like he did with Rahab, God extends a rescue cord to each of us."

 —**Jennifer Crosswhite,** author of the best-selling Christian romantic suspense *Protective Custody*

"Shadia Hrichi once again brings hope and challenge in a thrilling look at the life of Rahab. No matter your past or upbringing, Rahab teaches us what it means to trust, and walk, in faith with the unseen God, and how He can transform the seemingly insignificant into heroes of eternity."

 —**Tara Johnson,** author of *Engraved on the Heart*, *Where Dandelions Bloom*, and
  All Through the Night

"In *Rahab*, Shadia Hrichi explores details many of us have skimmed over for years—details that make a difference in how we read, understand, apply, and share Scripture as we eagerly await the day of Christ's return. Leading at a steady pace that encourages reflection, Shadia reveals how God uses a woman who might otherwise seem irrelevant. I enjoy how Shadia examines the stories of God's interactions with people who are often discarded or discredited as she teaches the foundational truths of Scripture in relevant and exciting ways. I can hardly wait to join Shadia on her next adventure through Scripture!"

 —**Xochitl Dixon,** contributing writer for *Our Daily Bread* and *God Hears Her*; author of the 2021
  ECPA Christian Book Award Children's Book Finalist, *Different Like Me*, and *Waiting for God*

"As she has done in her other outstanding Bible studies, Shadia Hrichi, in *Rahab*, has brought to life the story of a fascinating woman whose courage and faith in God transformed her own life and changed history. This book reveals God's surprising ways of accomplishing his purposes through people we might least expect. Who could have imagined that Rahab, a prostitute and woman without power or influence, would be able, through her belief in God, to save her family from destruction and end up in the ancestral line of Jesus? This Bible study goes in depth, putting Rahab's story in the context of the larger biblical narrative. Through the book's questions and exercises, readers in group or individually will be able to probe this amazing story's meaning and its relevance to their own lives and faith. Hrichi challenges her readers to live lives of courage and faith, and her book helps guide them in that direction."

—**Joseph Bentz,** author of *8 Old Testament Passages That Changed the World*

RAHAB

BEHIND THE SEEN

Exploring the Bible's Unsung Heroes

RAHAB

Rediscovering the God Who Saves Me

Shadia Hrichi

LEAFWOOD
PUBLISHERS

an imprint of Abilene Christian University Press

RAHAB
Rediscovering the God Who Saves Me

LEAFWOOD
P U B L I S H E R S
an imprint of Abilene Christian University Press

Copyright © 2023 by Shadia Hrichi

ISBN 978-1-68426-129-1 | LCCN 2023011205

Printed in the United States of America

ALL RIGHTS RESERVED

No part of this publication may be reproduced, stored in a retrieval system, or transmitted in any form by any means—electronic, mechanical, photocopying, recording, or otherwise—without prior written consent.

Scripture quotations, unless otherwise noted, are from The ESV® Bible (The Holy Bible, English Standard Version®) copyright © 2001 by Crossway, a publishing ministry of Good News Publishers. ESV® Text Edition: 2016. All rights reserved.

Scripture quotations marked NET are taken from the NET Bible® copyright © 1996–2017 All rights reserved. Build 30170414 by Biblical Studies Press, LLC.

Scripture quotations marked NIV are taken from The Holy Bible, New International Version®, NIV® copyright © 1973, 1978, 1984, 2011 by Biblica, Inc.® Used by permission. All rights reserved worldwide.

Scripture quotations marked NKJV are taken from the New King James Version® copyright © 1982 by Thomas Nelson. Used by permission. All rights reserved.

Scripture quotations marked NLT are taken from the Holy Bible, New Living Translation, copyright ©1996, 2004, 2007, 2015 by Tyndale House Foundation. Used by permission of Tyndale House Publishers, Inc., Carol Stream, IL 60188. All rights reserved.

LIBRARY OF CONGRESS CATALOGING-IN-PUBLICATION DATA
Names: Hrichi, Shadia, 1967- author.
Title: Rahab : rediscovering the God who saves me / Shadia Hrichi.
Description: Abilene, Texas : Leafwood Publishers, 2023. | Series: Behind the seen ; book 3
Identifiers: LCCN 2023011205 | ISBN 9781684261291 | ISBN 9781684268894 (ebook)
Subjects: LCSH: Rahab (Biblical figure—Textbooks.
Classification: LCC BS580.R3 H75 2023 | DDC 220.92—dc23/eng/20230602
LC record available at https://lccn.loc.gov/2023011205

Cover design by Thinkpen Design
Interior text design by Strong Design, Sandy Armstrong

Leafwood Publishers is an imprint of Abilene Christian University Press.
ACU Box 29138
Abilene, Texas 79699

1-877-816-4455
www.leafwoodpublishers.com

23 24 25 26 27 28 29 / 7 6 5 4 3 2 1

In loving memory of my mom:
Thank you for always believing in me.
I look forward to the day I will see you again in heaven.

"For everyone who calls on the name of the Lord will be saved."

Romans 10:13

CONTENTS

ACKNOWLEDGMENTS

It takes a village to write, publish, and launch a book. And what an amazing village God has gathered to release *Rahab* into the world!

With each new Bible study I write, God begins by bringing together a wonderful team of beta readers to work through the study, share feedback, and make suggestions. The *Rahab* beta readers team is no exception. My dear friends Sandi Miller and Linda Dunning have served as beta readers for every study I've written to date; I am so blessed! Sandi, in addition to your excellent feedback, you're the best "grammar police" an author could hope for; but it's your handwritten smiley faces, stars, and exclamation points that always make my day—thank you! And Linda, I especially appreciate your willingness to challenge me and offer feedback through the eyes of a group leader/facilitator; your contribution to the manuscript is always a blessing. And to Susan Cort Johnson, Holly Carmichael, Amanda Gardner, and Lisa Clement, thank you all for your willingness to step in and join the party. I am truly grateful for your gifts of time and your talents. Thank you for being on my beta readers team!

After writing the manuscript, off it goes to the fabulous publishing team at Leafwood Publishers. Jason Fikes, thank you for your expert developmental editing; Mary Hardegree, thank you for managing the editorial and production side of things; and AJ Hughes, thank you for your excellent copyedit. I'm also thrilled with Thinkpen Design for creating another stunning cover and with Sandy Armstrong of Strong Design for the fabulous interior design and typeset. However, putting a beautiful book together can only go so far without the help of a committed sales and marketing team. I appreciate all the hard work Duane Anderson and his team invest in helping each new Bible study find its place in the world. I am deeply honored to partner with each and every one of you.

Thank you to everyone who read an advanced copy of this study and offered your kind endorsement. Robin Lee Hatcher, I still chuckle that you decided we must be soul sisters after discovering we share an unfortunate tendency of killing our house plants. Thank you so much for your kind endorsement of this Bible study. And thank you to my sweet friend Francine Rivers for introducing Robin and me, as well as the added blessing of your own endorsement. Your friendship and enthusiastic support over the years have encouraged me more than you can imagine. I am also grateful to Joseph Bentz, Jennifer Crosswhite, Xochitl Dixon, and Tara Johnson. I love how God connected each one of us. Thank you for taking the time to read this Bible study; I know how busy each of you are. Your sacrifice of time and your wonderful endorsements are greatly appreciated!

Once a book is ready to publish, the next step is launch time! I am so thankful to the countless people who support me and the ministry through their love, prayers, gifts, and encouragement. I am blessed to have an incredible prayer team of over eighty people who pray faithfully and regularly for this ministry. Friends, your prayers are truly making a difference: from the *Hagar* Bible study being translated into Arabic to the truckloads of *Tamar* studies shipped to the Prison Book Project, God alone knows all the souls being impacted for the kingdom through your faithful prayers.

Thank you also to my wonderful church family, small group "sisters," and so many dear family and friends who have carried me through the past twelve months of writing this study while I faced some very difficult personal trials. Your love and prayers gave me the strength to press on; I can never thank you enough.

And what good would it do to have a new book launched into the world if it were not for the readers who choose to open its pages? To the person who is reading this right now, thank you for the privilege of serving you through words. There are many Bible studies you can choose from, and I am deeply humbled you have invited me—and *Rahab*—to be a part of your faith journey. It is my prayer that God would use this study to further fan into flame a holy joy for studying His Word.

Lastly, but most important of all, I give thanks to Jesus my King for saving me *from myself*. For taking my broken pieces and poor choices and fashioning them into something beautiful for Your kingdom purposes. I may never fully understand why You would choose me to teach Your glorious Word; but for as long as I am able, I will praise You for all you have done. It is my heartfelt prayer that the powerful truths in Rahab's story will draw many hearts to Your saving love.

To Your name alone be glory, honor, and praise forever!

ABOUT THE AUTHOR

SHADIA HRICHI IS A PASSIONATE BIBLE teacher, award-winning author, and speaker who has a heart for seeing lives transformed by the power of God's Word. Having experienced much heartache, such as a broken home, abortion, and divorce, Shadia captures the hearts of her audience as she illustrates God's love, faithfulness, and power of redemption through her personal experiences.

She received a master's degree in biblical and theological studies from Western Seminary, as well as a master's degree in criminal justice from the State University of New York. Shadia is the author of several Bible studies, including *Tamar*, *Legion*, and *Hagar*, all in her Behind the Seen series, and *Worthy of Love*, a story-driven Bible study for postabortion healing.

In addition to teaching Bible studies, Shadia is often invited to speak at churches, retreats, conferences, and other events. Her insightful and witty yet vulnerable teaching style reveals a compassion for the hurting, love for Jesus, and uncompromising commitment to the truth of God's Word. In addition to writing and speaking, Shadia has served on the faculty for a number of Christian writers conferences, and she provides workshops, coaching, and other resources for aspiring authors.

Currently residing in Northern California, Shadia loves to visit the ocean each week for "a date with Jesus." Be sure to visit www.shadiahrichi.com and join Shadia's "Brave the Deep" email community to receive Bible study tips, free resources, and updates on her writing. *Rahab* is the fourth study in her series, Behind the Seen: Exploring the Bible's Unsung Heroes. Be among the first to be notified of the next study!

ABOUT THE STUDY

WELCOME, FRIEND. I HOPE YOU ARE SITTING DOWN, because this study is sure to be a wild ride! I can hardly wait for us to begin our journey of *Rahab: Rediscovering the God Who Saves Me.*

This book is divided into six weeks, each comprising five days of personal study. For added flexibility, choose a commitment level that works best for you: "light" (15 minutes/day), "moderate" (30 minutes/day), "in-depth" (45 minutes/day) or "all-in" (60 minutes/day). See Group Study Tips (on the next page) for more details.

Each day of study includes one or more questions suitable for group discussion. These questions are followed by a ✿. Be sure not to overlook these questions, even if you are working through the material on your own. There are also Pause to Ponder sections throughout the study; these are designed to provide you with a time of personal reflection. Use the space in the margin (or, if you prefer, a journal or notebook) to respond to these questions. For readers desiring to dig even deeper, I've prepared Extra questions, which are preceded by a ❧.

At the end of each day, there is a Your Turn section for personal application. These questions are important. While studying the Bible can stir our hearts and open our eyes to wonderful truths, only when we apply what we have learned will it have a lasting impact for God's kingdom. In addition to this workbook, optional video teaching sessions are available at www.shadiahrichi.com/rahab.

During my study of Rahab, I often found myself fascinated by secondary topics related to the material. The Supplemental Readings I included throughout the study are not essential, but you may find them enjoyable and informative. I have included a section called Group Study Tips, which you may find useful if you are doing the study as a group.

One quick note: some paraphrase versions of the Bible may be inadequate for the purposes of this study. Whenever possible, it is recommended that you complete the exercises using a Bible translation that adheres to a more literal translation, such as the English Standard Version, New American Standard Bible, New King James Version, or King James Version.

Before you begin, take a few moments to ask the Holy Spirit to guide you over the next six weeks and to bless your commitment to this study. Then, as you open your Bible and your heart, begin each day with an eager expectation of *Rediscovering the God Who Saves Me.*

GROUP STUDY TIPS

BECAUSE ANY DEEP WORK OF GOD REQUIRES A SACRIFICE of time spent in His Word and in His presence, the volume of material in an in-depth study can be challenging for some participants. For this reason, several suggestions are provided to help you facilitate the study when participants have varying levels of time constraints.

Video Teaching Sessions

Seven optional video teaching sessions serve to complement and enhance the study. Watch Session One before you begin. Then, watch Session Two through Session Six before completing Week Two through Week Six in the study. Finally, watch Session Seven when you finish the study as a wrap-up. Sessions average between twenty and twenty-five minutes in length. Video sessions are available at www.shadiahrichi.com/rahab.

Plan an Extended Schedule

Instead of meeting for six weeks, allow two weeks for each chapter, for a total of twelve weeks. Every other week, invite participants to watch and discuss Shadia's video teaching sessions. These modifications will also provide periodic opportunities for participants to catch up on anything they may have missed or to spend extra time on areas of the study they may wish to explore further.

Customized Commitments for a Six-Week Schedule

Based on a six-week format, the following are suggested assignments based on an individual's time constraints:

For All Participants

- Read through each day's material, including the assigned Bible passages.
- Optional: read the Supplemental Reading section as provided in various weeks.

Light (15 Minutes a Day)

- Complete the Your Turn personal application section at the end of each day.
- If you have time, complete the Group Discussion questions, identified with a .

Moderate (30 Minutes a Day)

- Complete the various Pause to Ponder personal reflection sections as well as the Your Turn personal application section at the end of each day.
- Complete the Group Discussion questions identified with a .

In-Depth (45 Minutes a Day)

- Complete all questions except for the Extra questions identified with a .

All-In (60 Minutes a Day)

- Complete all the questions, including the Extra questions identified with a .
- Read all the Supplemental Reading sections.

May the Lord bless you as you journey through this study!

A NOTE FROM THE AUTHOR

THE STORY OF RAHAB HAS FASCINATED BIBLE STUDENTS and lay persons for centuries. Her story appears in a mere two chapters in the book of Joshua, and the events are curious right from the start. The book opens with God commissioning Joshua to lead the Israelites after the death of their leader Moses. Yet no sooner do the people come to the edge of the Promised Land than God puts the whole drama on hold to tell us the story of a Canaanite prostitute named Rahab. This interruption of the conquest story is not an accident, and it gives us our first glimpse into the theological significance of Rahab's story.

When we come to the New Testament, Rahab holds a surprisingly prominent position in several key faith passages. For starters, she is listed in the lineage of Christ! She even marries a prince! *The prostitute marries a prince!* This is the stuff of Hollywood movies and romance novels. The heartbeat of the Bible is God's passionate pursuit of His adulterous bride—a theme that echoes within the depths of every human heart.

I have a secret to share with you: Rahab's story is *our* story. It's a story centered on three key themes, without which there would be no Bible, no gospel, and no Savior. These themes are *faith*, *grace*, and *salvation*. Here is a woman who witnessed no miracles and knew none of God's laws. She merely heard of God's power and, in reverent fear, *believed*.

Through her daring faith, Rahab hid enemy spies, defied her king, risked her life, and found the living God. Rahab's story foreshadows events she could never have imagined. By the time you finish this study, you will never look at the story of Rahab the same way again. Are you ready? Let's rediscover the *God Who Saves Me*!

Your sister in Christ,

Shadia

Charm is deceitful, and beauty is vain,
but a woman who fears the LORD is to be praised.

Proverbs 31:30

PART I

THE PROMISE

WAITING FOR THE PROMISE OF
SALVATION

BEFORE TIME BEGAN, GOD MADE A PROMISE, AND WHETHER any of us realize it, all human history hinges on God's faithfulness to keep that promise. This week, we begin our study by tracing God's footsteps within the lives of His people; from the Garden of Eden to the edge of the Promised Land, we will see God at work, *behind the seen.*

DAY ONE
God Made a Promise

Long before Jesus stepped foot on the earth, before David was crowned king, before the walls of Jericho fell, before the Israelites crossed the Red Sea, before Noah built an ark, before Adam ate the fruit, or before the universe was spoken into being, God made a promise.

Read Titus 1:2 in the margin. What did God promise, and when did He make the promise?

"[We have this] hope of eternal life, which God, who never lies, promised before the ages began."
—Titus 1:2

What assurance do we have that God will keep His promise?

Why does His promise matter?

Why does it matter to *you*?

God could have promised anything—or nothing—before creating the world. This means that long before you took your first step or even your first breath, long before God planted you in your mother's womb or you chose to go your own way, God, in His mercy, promised the "hope of eternal life."

PAUSE TO PONDER

Think of a time when someone made a promise to you that you held dear, only to discover the other person let you down. How did you feel? How did it change you, or what did you learn? How can you take comfort in knowing that God, who never lies, always keeps His promises?

All the way back at the beginning of human history, in the Garden of Eden, God announced that a Savior would be born of human descent.

To fulfill His promise, God announced at the beginning of human history, in the Garden of Eden, that a Savior would be born of human descent (Gen. 3:15). Some of the people whom God would choose to weave into the Savior's ancestry are the last people we might expect—like Rahab, whose story is at the heart of this study. Her story is found in the Old Testament book of Joshua, which recounts the events following the Exodus—namely, after God raised up Moses to lead the Hebrew slaves out of Egypt and miraculously divided the Red Sea. This enabled God's people to head into the land He promised to Abraham so many generations before. When Moses died, leadership of the people passed to Joshua, Moses's faithful assistant. It was Joshua who would lead their continued quest toward the Promised Land.

However, before we embark on Rahab's entrance into the story, we need to take some time to look at several key events that lead up to the book of Joshua where Rahab first appears. This will provide us with important context and help us to see her story in proper perspective. The first key event took place all the way back in the Garden of Eden, after Adam and Eve made the tragic choice to disobey God's one (and only!) command (Gen. 2:17, 3:17). It is here where God, in His mercy, announced His promise of a Savior. While this was certainly good news, Adam and Eve were nevertheless banished from their garden paradise (yet even this is evidence of God's mercy[1]). From there, it did not take long for the human race, and sin, to begin to fill the earth.

Just three chapters later, in Genesis 6, the fallout from mankind's sin and rebellion reached the point where God had had enough. All but eight descendants of Adam and Eve perished in a worldwide flood.[2] But there was one man, Noah, who "found favor in the eyes of the LORD" (Gen. 6:8). God then waited ten generations after saving Noah and his family to introduce us to a man named Abraham.[3] It was through him that the Savior of the world would one day come. Little did Abraham know that a day was coming when God would bless him with a promise that seemed all but impossible.

Facing the Impossible

Several years ago, I prayed a prayer that seemed all but impossible. It was Palm Sunday weekend. I was attending a writers conference in the beautiful redwood forest of Mount Hermon in Northern California. Just weeks prior, I had completed the manuscript for my Bible study on Hagar and sent it to my publisher. With the book deadline off my shoulders, I was eager for the opportunity to relax and enjoy time with friends at the conference. On Saturday night before Palm Sunday, we all filed into the auditorium to enjoy a time of singing and to hear a message from the keynote speaker. About halfway through the message, the speaker challenged his audience of writers and authors to "pray boldly" concerning the writing ministry God had entrusted to each one of us. Something about the challenge resonated with me: bold prayers, when offered up in faith, honor God.

I went to bed that night pondering the challenge to pray boldly. I woke only a few hours later, long before the sun began to rise. I sensed this was God's invitation to spend some quiet time with Him. Grateful that my room had a coffee maker, I got up, made a cup of coffee, pulled the thick comforter off the bed, and headed out to the small balcony. I sat down and breathed in the crisp mountain air while warming my hands on my steaming mug. With only the sound of nighttime insects on the ground below and a few birds rustling in the trees above, I soaked in the silence and began to pray.

Bold prayers, when offered up in faith, honor God.

I poured my heart out to God, and I shared my earnest desire to see the *Hagar* Bible study minister to souls who needed a reminder that God sees them. As I did, the challenge to "pray boldly" returned to my thoughts, but I'll be honest with you: I didn't know how to respond. What bold prayer would be pleasing to God? Should I focus on the ministry? On reaching more readers? On outreach? On pursuing every writer's dream of quitting their day job and writing full-time? Finally, not knowing what else to do, I simply prayed, "God, I do not know what to pray for, but I know that bold prayers honor You. Please show me what bold prayer concerning this ministry You want me to pray." God wasted no time. Immediately, I sensed His Holy Spirit press on my heart to pray that the *Hagar* study would be translated and published in Arabic.

Honestly, I do not know what I expected God's answer to be, but that wasn't it. Translated? Arabic? Did I hear Him correctly? After all, not even the English version had been published yet. Aren't books translated years later? If at all? And . . . Arabic? Really? Isn't Spanish typically the next step?

But God's voice was clear. So, I prayed.

Slowly, the sun began to rise. It was Palm Sunday. Later that morning, I shared my prayer with close friends and mentors at the conference. When I returned home, I shared the story with my ministry prayer team, my Bible study group, and my publisher—asking everyone to join me in this bold prayer. Through a series of events only God could orchestrate, just six months after *Hagar* was published, I could hardly believe that I was holding in my hands a printed copy of the Bible study translated into Arabic, which was being distributed to churches across Egypt and throughout the Middle East.

PAUSE TO PONDER

Describe a seemingly impossible situation where you felt challenged to pray a bold prayer. What did you pray? What was the outcome? Were you encouraged? Disappointed? What did you learn? In the end, what impact did it have on your faith or your relationship with God? If you cannot think of a time when you prayed a bold prayer, what may be holding you back?

Choosing to Believe

Read Genesis 11:29–30 and 12:1–7. In addition to God's gracious promises in Genesis 12:2–3, what else did God promise to Abraham, according to Genesis 12:7?

Compare and contrast Genesis 11:30 with 12:7. What challenge did the elderly Abraham face, and how did he respond?

Next, read Genesis 15:1–6, which took place roughly ten years later.

What was Abraham's heartache?

What was God's assurance to Abraham?

How did Abraham respond?

Imagine being in Abraham's sandals. How else could Abraham have responded? List as many responses as you can think of.

What can you learn from Abraham's example in Genesis 15:1–6 (see also Genesis 12:7)?

"Is anything too hard for the Lord?" —Genesis 18:14

Although both Abraham and Sarah were advanced in years and Sarah was barren, God assured Abraham that he would indeed have a son. In fact, God promised Abraham descendants as numerous as the stars. Instead of arguing with God, focusing on what he lacked, asking God for a sign, or despairing over his seemingly impossible circumstances, we read simply that Abraham "believed the Lord, and [as a result, God] counted it to him as righteousness" (Gen. 15:6). Against all human logic, against impossible odds, Abraham made a choice: he "believed the Lord."

Read Genesis 17:1–8. What else did God promise to give to Abraham, according to the following verses? I completed one for you.

Genesis 17:4:

Genesis 17:6:

Genesis 17:7: *God will establish an everlasting covenant between Abraham and his descendants: to be his God and God to his descendants.*

Genesis 17:8:

That's a lot of promises! But one thing God did not promise was that the road to the Promised Land would be an easy one.

..................................YOUR TURN..................................

Where in your life right now do you sense God is calling you to trust Him?

What bold prayer do you need to bring to God today?

If you're not sure, ask Him; God delights in honest conversation. Write your prayer below.

Day Two
Facing Your Fears

Yesterday, we began our study by being reminded of the incredible promise God made before time began.

Refresh your memory by filling in the blanks with the missing word or phrase from Titus 1:2.

We have this "hope of ________________, which God, who never ________, promised before the ages began."

Read Genesis 15:12–14. Briefly summarize the passage in your own words.

Along with God's promise to Abraham came some difficult news. The fulfillment of His promise to give Abraham's offspring the land of Canaan would be preceded by four hundred years of slavery. That does not sound encouraging, but Abraham was looking beyond the earthly promises to something far greater.

Read Hebrews 11:1–2. How is faith described, according to verse 1?

Read Hebrews 11:6 in the margin. List two or three ways people try to earn God's favor, in your experience.

"...for whoever would draw near to God must believe that he exists and that he rewards those who seek him." —Hebrews 11:6

How might these efforts to earn God's favor grieve His heart? (Hint: see Ephesians 2:8–9.)

"Some trust in chariots and some in horses, but we trust in the name of the LORD our God."

—Psalm 20:7

In one of my favorite books, theologian A. W. Tozer explains, "Unbelief is actually perverted faith, for it puts its trust not in the living God but in dying men."[4]

Spend a few moments meditating on Tozer's words, along with Psalm 20:7 written in the margin. How have you seen these principles at work? In the table, write some examples of trusting in people or trusting in God based on your own experiences. Complete as many as you can think of. I included one of my own as an example.

	Trust in People	**Trust in God**
Your culture		
Your church		*Our church has an annual "faith promise" pledge whereby the church as a whole, and members individually, prayerfully commit funds to support missions work for the next year, having faith that God will enable us to keep our promise/pledge.*
Your home/family		
Your personal life		

Of the examples you shared, which one captures your attention the most? Why?

Misplaced Faith

The truth is that every human being lives by faith—in someone. Before you or I put our faith in God, we placed our faith in someone else. Often, that person was the one looking back at us in the mirror, trusting in our own ideas of how the world operates, our place in it, and our ideas of what would make us happy.

Read Hebrews 11:8-10 and 11:13. List the challenges Abraham faced as a result of his obedience.

Abraham "died in faith" (Heb. 11:13) without seeing God's promises fulfilled. What was Abraham looking forward to, according to Hebrews 11:10 (see also 11:16)?

PAUSE TO PONDER

How about you? How often on average do you take time to reflect on the heavenly home that God promises to all who belong to Him?

weekly   monthly   rarely   I have never done this

When you reflect on your heavenly home, in what ways does it impact your time with God? What impact does it have on your outlook on life in general? If you rarely or have never done this, why not try incorporating this into your prayer time this week? Come back and record in what ways, if any, it had an impact on your time with God or on your outlook on life.

Abraham never saw the fulfillment of God's promise in his lifetime; rather, his faith was anchored in what lies beyond this life. Yet, at the same time, God had made a promise to give Abraham's descendants a land to call their own, and God always keeps His promises. However, as we read at the end of the lesson from yesterday, the road to the Promised Land would not be an easy one. Let's take a quick look at several events leading up to the birth of Moses—the man God would task with leading His people to the Promised Land.

God's promise passed on to Abraham's son Isaac, then to Isaac's son Jacob, who fathered twelve sons. Sadly, Jacob's special affection toward his young son Joseph resulted in no small amount of jealousy among Joseph's older brothers, so much so that a band of the brothers resorted to selling Joseph into slavery and allowing their father to believe Joseph was dead.

But as Joseph was being carried away to Egypt, he was not alone. God was with Joseph. In fact, Joseph eventually rose to power in Egypt and, in time, found himself second in command after Pharaoh himself. Roughly twenty years went by, after which God sent a famine throughout the land. This turned out to be a blessing because it led Jacob and his sons and their entire tribe to Egypt, where they were unexpectedly reunited with Joseph. Not only were the brothers reconciled, but symbolically speaking, Jacob received his son Joseph back from the dead.[5] All would seem well and good except for one thing: God's promise to give Abraham's descendants a land of their own had yet to be fulfilled. Little did anyone know that Egypt would become the nation where God's people would suffer the four hundred years of slavery God foretold to Abraham just three generations prior.

Read Genesis 50:24–26.

What did Joseph place his faith in? (What hope was he clinging to?)

What promise did Joseph require from his brothers?

Why do you suppose this was so important to Joseph?

Eventually, Jacob and all his sons died in the land of Egypt. Their descendants, however, continued to thrive and multiply, but a new king was soon to take Egypt's throne.

There's a New King in Town

Perhaps you are familiar with the biblical story of the Exodus. Roughly four hundred years after Jacob's descendants were enslaved in Egypt, Moses was born. Though he was a Hebrew, he was reared by the daughter of Egypt's king. When he grew up, he ran away, only to return years later as one sent by God to free the Hebrew people from their slavery. But the book of Exodus does not begin with the birth of Moses. It begins with a profound but underappreciated story of incredible courage.

Read Exodus 1:1–10. What was the king of Egypt afraid of?

Read Exodus 1:11–14. Summarize the events.

It is at this point that most reenactments or retellings of the Exodus story skip ahead to Exodus 1:22, where we read, "Then Pharaoh commanded all his people, 'Every son that is born to the Hebrews you shall cast into the Nile, but you shall let every daughter live.'" The story then immediately dives into the birth of Moses.

However, when we consider the fact that so much of the Bible involves the continuous human struggle between fear and faith, it is unfortunate that the events in Exodus 1:15–21 are often glossed over. I assure you: the story recorded in those seven verses and the life lessons we can glean from them are ones you do not want to miss! And if that doesn't get you excited, just wait until you see the parallels to these verses that we will uncover when we reach Rahab's entrance into the story. But I'm getting ahead of myself.

Read Exodus 1:15–16. What was the king's aim?

Who did the king turn to in order to help him carry out his plan?

Do you find the king's choice surprising? Why or why not?

Picture the scene. At the time of these events, Egypt was one of the most imposing nations on earth, possessing both great political and military power.[6] The kings of Egypt (or pharaohs) were considered by the people—and themselves—to be gods. When the king of Egypt feared that the Hebrews were growing too large in number, rather than sending out his army or summoning his local officials, he called two lowly Hebrew midwives. Really? That's your plan, O mighty king of Egypt?

The story is curious right from the start. Notice also that the midwives are named. This is another intriguing aspect of the story. After all, it could have simply read, *Then the king of Egypt said to the Hebrew midwives, "When you serve as midwife to the Hebrew women . . ."* But God chose to include the midwives' personal names, ensuring that the courageous choices of these two women would be recounted for generations. Speaking of names, I did some research to see what I could discover about these two Hebrew names. My efforts did not disappoint. It turns out that the name Shiphrah means "beautiful, *prolific*, or to procreate,"[7] and Puah means "splendor, light, or child bearing—specifically in relation to *parents' joy*."[8] Isn't that interesting?

The Fear of the Lord

Read Exodus 1:17. What reason is given for the midwives' willful disregard of the king's order?

How would you describe what it means to "fear the Lord" to someone who does not know God?

Read Job 28:28 and Proverbs 8:13 in the margin. How do these verses shed light on your understanding of what it means to "fear the Lord"?

The root Hebrew word translated "fear" (twice in Exodus 1) is *yare*. When used in the context of fearing God, it relates to having a humble reverence toward and healthy fear of God. Because God is infinitely wise and powerful, any sane person would immediately recognize that we *should* fear God. However, those who know Him personally quickly discover that He is also infinitely loving and kind and desires the best for us. After all, He tenderly and intentionally created each one of us in His own image.

"... the fear of the Lord, that is wisdom, and to turn away from evil is understanding."
—Job 28:28

"The fear of the Lord is hatred of evil."
—Proverbs 8:13

Why is it wise for us to fear (*yare*) God?

How is this different from being afraid of God?

Where in your life right now are you grateful in knowing that God is infinitely wise, powerful, and "greatly to be feared" (Ps. 89:7)?

Where in your life right now do you need a greater "fear of the LORD" (that is, a humble reverence toward God and healthy fear of Him)? Write a prayer of confession, gratitude, or petition (or all three!) as God leads you.

DAY THREE
A Step of Faith

Yesterday, we learned that the Hebrew midwives, Shiphrah and Puah, "feared God and did not do as the king of Egypt commanded them" (Exod. 1:17). Imagine that you are one of these two women summoned to stand in the presence of one of the most powerful rulers of the known world. Even more, he is the ruler of the land in which you are now living—as a foreign slave. You have no idea why the king would summon you. After all, you are just a midwife. Your mind races with the possible scenarios—none of them good. You take comfort in knowing that your friend and partner in midwifery is going with you. That, and the fact that your family, along with the whole Hebrew community, is praying for you as you and your friend make your way to Pharaoh's palace.

All too soon you find yourselves standing together before the king. Of all the scenarios that play out in your mind, you could never imagine what this arrogant king would demand. He asks you to do the unthinkable. He wants you to murder newborn infants—a heinous sin against God and in direct opposition to your life's

"...here is the conclusion of the matter: Fear God and keep his commandments, for this is the duty of all mankind."
—Ecclesiastes 12:13 NIV

work and calling. Does the king realize what he is asking? How can he expect you to violate your people, your conscience, and your God?

PAUSE TO PONDER

Have you ever found yourself in a situation where you were asked to do something that went against a core personal belief? What were the risks? How did you respond? What was the outcome? Did it impact your relationship with God? If so, how?

Read Exodus 1:18–20 and then answer the following questions:

When Pharaoh summoned the midwives a second time and demanded an explanation for their disobedience, what was their answer?

How would you describe Shiphrah and Puah's actions? Wise? Reckless? Courageous? Something else?

Explain your response.

There is nothing in the passage (or anywhere else in Scripture) to suggest that what the women stated was true. Even so, what was God's response to the midwives' choice to defy the king of Egypt?

What general principle do you see at work here regarding how we are to respond when faced with a conflict between government's laws and God's laws?

"We must obey God rather than men." —Acts 5:29

"If you see the extortion of the poor, or perversion of justice and fairness in the government, do not be astonished by the matter. For the high official is watched by a higher official, and there are higher ones over them!"

—Ecclesiastes 5:8 NET

The king surely underestimated the midwives. Rather than succumbing to fear for their lives (the threat of death would have been all too real), Shiphrah and Puah responded out of a reverent fear of God.

What else did God do according to the last segment of Exodus 1:20?

Compare and contrast the end of Exodus 1:20 with verses 9–10 earlier in the chapter. Do you see any irony at work here?

Explain.

God was just getting started. Read Exodus 1:21. How did God reward the midwives?

Ponder God's choice of reward. Do you find it curious? Encouraging? Surprising? Explain your response.

I do not know about you, but I find this to be a beautiful picture of poetic justice. After all, we read at the beginning of the chapter that the king feared the Hebrew people because they were multiplying. Then the king commanded the midwives to slow down the population rate (which the women ignored). Instead, we read that the people increased all the more. On top of that, as if to mock Egypt's king, God turned around and blessed the midwives with families of their own—adding even more to their number!

In yesterday's lesson, we learned that Shiphrah means "beautiful, prolific, or to procreate" and Puah means "splendor, light, or child bearing—specifically in relation to parents' joy." When we consider the meaning of Shiphrah and Puah's names, along with God's blessing of granting them families of their own (implying

When you or I find the courage to take a stand against evil, we can trust that God stands with us.

that they previously had no children), we see the beauty of God at work, not only in the lives of the Hebrew people as a whole, but in individual lives as well. I love the fact that God is so personal. He takes notice of every detail of our lives. In the case of Shiphrah and Puah, God made a point to honor the faith of these two women who found the courage to stand up to the mighty king of Egypt, who trusted that the one true King stood with them. Oh, I can hardly wait for you to see the surprising way these events tie directly into Rahab's story!

PAUSE TO PONDER

What do you suppose our world might be like if more of God's people had the faith and courage of Shiphrah and Puah? How about in your church? What impact might your church have in its community if all of its members made courageous, God-fearing choices? How about you? What difference could you make in your workplace, neighborhood, or family?

A Tragic Turn

Sadly, after God blessed the midwives, the story took a violent turn.

Read Exodus 1:22. Who did Pharaoh commission to do his dirty work? Be specific.

Do you suppose there might have been some people who disobeyed the king's command? Explain.

Let's suppose some of the Egyptian people chose to disobey the king. What motivations might have been behind their decision not to participate in the slaughter? List as many as you can think of. (Note: as the response calls for speculation, there are no right or wrong answers.)

The king of Egypt took matters into his own hands by demanding that "all his people" take part in his paranoid attempt to keep the Hebrew population at a level that didn't threaten his personal insecurities. Scripture does not tell us that every citizen willingly participated in the slaughter. Based on Exodus 12:38, which we will briefly explore tomorrow, we know that some of the people chose to seek refuge in the God of Israel. As such, it is reasonable to surmise that not all the people of Egypt took part in the slaughter of the male Hebrew children. Perhaps some were sympathetic to the Hebrews' plight. Others may have viewed the Pharaoh's demands as going too far. Yet, in the midst of the horror, God did not abandon His people. He raised up one man, Moses.

Most of us are familiar with this part of the story: Moses was rescued as an infant from the Nile River by Pharoah's daughter, who raised him as her own son. When Moses grew up, his compassion for the plight of his Hebrew brothers and sisters led him to rescue a Hebrew from an Egyptian taskmaster, whom Moses murdered and buried in the sand (Exod. 2:1–12). When Pharaoh heard of it, he wanted Moses dead. Fearing for his life, Moses fled to the land of Midian, where he settled, married, and raised a family (Exod. 2:13–22).

Meanwhile, the Hebrew people continued to suffer in Egypt. Then one day, Moses experienced a miraculous desert encounter that would alter the trajectory of his life forever.

> Read Exodus 3:1–10. Verses 7–8 are printed below. This is a portion of the message God spoke to Moses from the burning bush. Fill in the missing words based on the passage.
>
> Then the Lord said, "I have surely _________ the affliction of my people who are in Egypt and have ___________ their cry because of their taskmasters. I __________ their sufferings, and I have come down to ________________ them out of the hand of the Egyptians and to bring them up out of that land to a good and broad land, a land flowing with milk and honey, to the place of the Canaanites, the Hittites, the Amorites, the Perizzites, the Hivites, and the Jebusites."

After the people of God had suffered as slaves in Egypt for over four hundred years, God announced that the time had come to set them free. God then began to pummel Egypt with a series of ten plagues. At the pronouncement of the seventh plague, something interesting happened.

Read Exodus 9:18-26 (optional: read Exodus 9:13-26). Write verse 20 below.

Compare Exodus 9:20 with Exodus 9:21. What difference did "fear[ing] the word of the LORD" (Exod. 9:20) make, and for whom?

What general leadership principle can you glean from these events? (Hint: see Proverbs 29:2 in the margin.)

The root Hebrew word translated "feared" in Exodus 9:20 is *yare*. It's the same root word we encountered yesterday in Exodus 1 in our exploration of the driving force behind the midwives' decision to defy the king. This Hebrew word appears roughly sixty-five times in the Old Testament. Except for a handful of verses, the word is nearly always used in direct reference to having a reverential fear of God.

We might be tempted to think that our faith and reverence for God is strictly a personal matter, but as we are discovering, nothing could be further from the truth. In the case of Pharaoh's officials, the lives of their slaves were at stake. In the case of the Hebrew midwives, the lives of newborn children were at stake. At the end of the day, all of us are impacted by the choices of others, and others are impacted by the choices we make. While we cannot control other people's decisions, we can choose, like Shiphrah and Puah, what will control ours.

................................YOUR TURN................................

Think of someone you know who seems to have an exceptionally reverent fear of God. What do you suppose contributes to him or her having a strong but healthy fear of God?

If you are not sure, consider reaching out to the person and asking what has helped foster his or her view of God. Come back and share what you learned.

What might your life look like one year from now if all your decisions from this point forward flowed out of a reverent fear of God?

What one step will you take this week to move toward having a stronger, healthy fear of God?

If you sense something is standing in the way, bring your honest struggles to God in prayer. Write what He reveals to you.

DAY FOUR
Taking the Road Less Traveled

Several years ago, I flew from California to Cincinnati to speak for a pregnancy center banquet that same night. The plan was for me to pick up a rental car at the Cincinnati airport and drive to the church where I would speak. On the flight, I sat next to a tall, kind man who I guessed was in his early sixties. We chatted a bit. He told me about his daughter and grandchildren and the church he attended. *What a blessing to be seated next to a fellow churchgoer,* I thought. When he asked about what brought me to Cincinnati, I explained I was speaking that night at a fundraiser just outside the city. He remarked that we'd be landing at around 4 p.m., the height of rush hour traffic, and he offered to take a look at the directions I printed. (Knowing my painfully inadequate sense of direction, I printed directions just in case the GPS didn't work.) I handed him the slip of paper. The look on his face spelled trouble.

"You'll never make it in time going this way. Downtown Cincinnati is a bear during rush hour." He took out a pen and started writing new directions on the back of the paper. His route looked far simpler than the directions I printed. "Look, I actually work at the airport; I'm a pilot; I'm off duty and on my way home. The airport is large; it will take you at least fifteen minutes to get to the rental car desk, but I know a shortcut." Having worked a number of years at an airport myself (not as a pilot, mind you—with my sense of direction, navigating a car is dangerous enough), I knew there were shortcuts here and there that enabled one to avoid the crowded masses.

After we landed and exited the gateway, he kindly ushered me through the less-traveled hallways, and, in barely three minutes, I was standing at the rental car desk. Those extra few minutes I saved, along with the pilot's directions that steered me away from rush hour traffic, allowed me time to enjoy a brief stopover at the hotel to freshen up before heading to the event.

When God sends someone to lead you in a different direction, it pays to listen.

Shedding the Chains of Slavery

Read Exodus 12:1–14 and 12:21–23 (optional: read all of Exodus 12). Briefly summarize the events.

One devastating plague after another, the last of which was the most severe of all: God would strike dead all firstborn males throughout the land. But the Israelites were given an escape. Through Moses, God instructed the people to cover the doorposts of their homes with lamb's blood. By doing so, God promised His people that the angel of death would pass over them when He struck the land of Egypt by killing all firstborn males.

Read Exodus 12:29–32 and 12:37–38 (optional: read all of Exodus 12:29–42). When the Israelites left Egypt, Scripture records that a "mixed multitude" (Exod. 12:38) went with them. Who might this "mixed multitude" represent? List as many possibilities as you can think of.

Why do you suppose this "mixed multitude" wanted to go with the Israelites? Once again, list as many reasons as you can think of. (As these responses call for speculation, there are no right or wrong answers.)

Of the reasons you listed above, which one stands out or stirs your heart the most? Why?

This "mixed multitude" may have comprised Egyptian citizens as well as other people groups, perhaps other slaves, who, after seeing the great signs of the one true God, decided to attach themselves to the Israelites and follow their God. Rather than following the crowd of Egyptians listening to Pharaoh, here were those who chose to go a different direction, to follow a different voice. Based on the passage we will study next, it seems that God was pleased to welcome them.

PAUSE TO PONDER

Describe a time when you sensed God leading you to step away from following the crowd. Perhaps it was a situation at work or school or even at church. Did you follow God's voice? If so, what gave you the courage, and what was the outcome? If you went along with the crowd, what was the result, and what did you learn? Finally, what advice would you give to someone who feels they are being pulled in two different directions?

Read Exodus 12:43-44 and 12:48-49. Apart from the Israelites, who else was invited to participate in the Passover, and what were the conditions?

Glance back at God's promise to Abraham in Genesis 12:3, and contrast it with Exodus 12:43-44 and 12:48-49. How do you see God's promise to Abraham beginning to take shape?

God loves all people. This has been true from the beginning. When God freed the Israelites from their slavery, He instructed Moses to institute the Passover, a vivid reminder of God's mercy and deliverance. Even foreigners were welcome to participate in the Passover, provided that they identified themselves with God's people and committed themselves to following God's commands and covenant.

Fill in the missing words and phrases from Exodus 12:43 and 48 printed below.

And the LORD said to Moses and Aaron, "This is the statute of the Passover . . . If a __________ shall sojourn with you and would keep the Passover to the LORD, let all his males be circumcised. Then he may ___________ and keep it; he shall be as a native of the land."

Wow! They "shall be as a native of the land" (Exod. 12:48). Given the importance of national identity at that time, this was quite remarkable. But we see this picture of God's heart throughout Scripture. How deeply God loves us. How far He pursues us. From the beginning, His plan of salvation welcomes all who come to Him.

The Journey Has Just Begun

Regardless of how much (or little) time you have spent at a church or reading your Bible, I imagine you have heard of the Exodus story. In brief, it is here where the Israelites pack up and head out of Egypt, but just as they are gaining headway, Pharaoh changes his mind and pursues the Israelites until they find themselves trapped, filled with fear, between Pharaoh's army and the Red Sea. Just when it seems all is lost, God divides the raging Red Sea so that His people can cross over to freedom while the army of Egypt pursues them and drowns.

It's a sobering yet beautiful picture of God's desire to free His people from slavery. However, the journey to the Promised Land was just beginning. After God miraculously delivered the Israelites from Egypt by parting the Red Sea (Exod.14), the Israelites witnessed even more miracles. Let's take a quick look at a few. This will provide us with greater perspective when we examine what happens next.

For each passage describing the miracles, complete the sentence using one of the following keywords. I completed the first one for you.

serpent   rock   victory   heaven   water

God made the bitter _water_ sweet so that the people could drink. (Exod. 15:22–25)

God gave His people bread from __________ to eat. (Exod. 16:2–4)

God brought gushing water from the ___________. (Exod. 17:1–7)

God gave His people _____________ over their enemies. (Exod. 17:8–13)

God instructed Moses to lift up a bronze ___________ so that whoever looked upon it was saved from the deadly snakes. (Num. 21:4–9)

Glance back at Exodus 15:22–26. How did the Lord describe Himself, according to verse 26?

What principle was the Lord trying to teach His people in this passage?

Glance back at Exodus 17:8–16. How did Moses describe the Lord, according to verse 15?

What principle was the Lord trying to teach His people in this passage?

The people of God witnessed miracle after miracle after miracle—and we looked at only a few!

Read Exodus 31:18–32:6. While God was meeting with Moses on Mount Sinai, what did the Israelites do in Moses's absence? Circle all that apply.

Sang songs to the Lord

Demanded gods be made for them

Studied God's law

Declared that a golden calf brought them out of Egypt

Made sacrifices to a golden calf

Ate, drank, and partied

Interesting Fact: Many years later, when Hezekiah was king of Judah, he destroyed Moses's bronze serpent, which the Israelites had kept and later worshiped as an idol. (See 2 Kings 18:4.)

Perhaps like me, you've heard someone say, "If God would just reveal Himself to me, then I will believe." Do the events we have studied so far align with the above assumption?

Explain.

When the Israelites neared the Promised Land, Moses sent twelve spies into the land of Canaan, one man from each of the twelve tribes. After forty days, the spies returned, and all but two of them give a bad report, stirring up fear among the people. Only Joshua and Caleb urged the people to have faith that God would enable them to take the land (Num. 13). Sadly, the people chose fear over faith and responded by demanding that Joshua and Caleb be stoned. Although God stepped in to protect His two faithful witnesses (Num. 14:6–10), as a result of the people's refusal to enter the Promised Land, the Israelites spent the next forty years wandering in the wilderness until all in that generation died except for Joshua and Caleb.

························YOUR TURN·····························

Imagine if you had been among the Israelites, witnessing all these miracles.

What impact do you suppose it would have had on your faith?

How have you witnessed God's faithfulness to you this past week?

Thinking again on the past week, in what ways have you responded in fear over faith? To put it another way: Where are you currently walking by sight rather than by faith?

Bring your praises, along with your struggles, to God in prayer. Thank Him for His faithfulness to you this week, and confess the areas where you are struggling. Ask Him to show you what is holding you back from trusting Him and what it would look like to walk by faith rather than by sight. Write your prayer below.

DAY FIVE
Standing on the Edge of the Promised Land

Yesterday, we left our story with the tragic reality of the Israelites' refusal to enter the Promised Land out of fear, resulting in a forty-year aimless trek in the wilderness. But God was watching—and working. During this time, God recognized Joshua for his faith and set him apart to become Moses's assistant. After the Israelites crossed the Red Sea, Joshua was the one who was entrusted to lead the Israelites. Finally, when it came time for Moses to breathe his last, it was Joshua whom God appointed to succeed Moses as leader of the people (Num. 27:12–20; Deut. 31:7–23, 34:7–9).

In the Bible, the book of Joshua is preceded by five books: Genesis, Exodus, Leviticus, Numbers, and Deuteronomy. Collectively, these five books are often referred to as The Law, The Law of Moses, the Book of the Law, and are also known as Torah in the Hebrew Bible. The book of Joshua is considered the first book of the "Prophets"[9] (see Luke 24:44).

The book of Joshua opens with: "After the death of Moses the servant of the LORD, the LORD said to Joshua the son of Nun, Moses' assistant, 'Moses my servant is dead'" (Josh. 1:1–2).

How's that for a pep talk?

Imagine being among the people of Israel when you learned that Moses had died. How may this have impacted

your courage to move forward?

Explain.

The first five books of the Bible are called Torah in the Hebrew Bible (meaning "law, instruction, or direction") and are referred to as the Pentateuch in Greek (meaning "five books").

your faith in God?

Explain.

The truth is that the death of Moses could easily have rattled the people's courage and even their faith. After all, Moses had been their leader for over forty years! Not only that, but they had witnessed God performing miracle after miracle through Moses. Would they be faithful to follow Joshua as their new leader?

After reminding Joshua of Moses's death, the Lord continued His message to Joshua: "Now therefore arise, go over this Jordan, you and all this people, into the land that I am giving to them, to the people of Israel. Every place that the sole of your foot will tread upon I have given to you, just as I promised to Moses" (Josh. 1:2–3).

Despite the people's repeated rebellion, grumbling, and disobedience, God reaffirmed His promise to lead His people over the Jordan River and into the Promised Land. It is here where we witness God's truth in action that even "if we are faithless, he remains faithful—for he cannot deny himself" (2 Tim. 2:13). Even though Moses had died, God made a promise to Abraham that his descendants would live in the Promised Land—and God always keeps His promises.

PAUSE TO PONDER

Read 2 Timothy 2:13 in the margin. Reflect on the past week. Is there an area in which you have been struggling to remain faithful (perhaps being rebellious, grumbling, or disobedient)? Take a few moments and ponder all the ways you have experienced God's faithfulness this past week. Write a prayer of gratitude (and perhaps surrender) as God leads.

Be Strong and Courageous

In the book of Joshua, there is perhaps no better-known verse than Joshua 1:9, where the Lord encouraged Joshua, "Be strong and courageous. Do not be frightened, and do not be dismayed, for the LORD your God is with you wherever you go."

The verse is so popular that curiosity led me to conduct an Internet search to see how many graphics and memes there are quoting Joshua 1:9. I quickly realized that there are too many to count. In addition, I found ornaments, wall

---

"[Even] if we are faithless, He remains faithful—for he cannot deny himself."

—2 Timothy 2:13

Interesting Fact: The Hebrew name Joshua (*Yeshua*, or its longer form, *Yehoshua*) has its counterpart in the Greek name Jesus (*Iesous*).[10] Both mean "Yahweh saves."

art, coffee mugs, T-shirts, key chains—even tattoos. The popularity of the verse is not surprising, especially given our cultural craving for and admiration of individual success, courage, and power. Who doesn't need some encouragement now and then?

Read Joshua 1:1-9, which records the words the Lord spoke to Joshua after Moses had died. What was the Lord's commission to Joshua, according to verses 2–3?

How many times does the phrase "be strong and courageous" appear in verses 2–9?

Why do you suppose the Lord repeated this exhortation? List as many reasons as you can think of.

In ancient languages like Hebrew, there are no punctuation marks, uppercase versus lowercase letters, or different fonts to add emphasis to a text. Repeating a phrase once would add some emphasis. Stating it a third time was the author's way of saying, *You do not want to miss this!*

The phrase "be strong and courageous" is found in verses 6, 7, and 9. But the Lord's exhortation to Joshua also includes a lengthy passage sandwiched within these verses. However, these middle verses seem far less popular. Let's see if we can discover why.

Reread Joshua 1:7b-8, which is printed below. Underline every direct or indirect reference to God's law, as well as obeying, remembering, meditating on, or following the law.

. . . being careful to do according to all the law that Moses my servant commanded you. Do not turn from it to the right hand or to the left, that you may have good success wherever you go. This Book of the Law shall not depart from your mouth, but you shall meditate on it day and night, so that you may be careful to do according to all that is written in it. For then you will make your way prosperous, and then you will have good success.

Consider the oft-quoted verse 9 within the context of the full exhortation of verses 6–9. What difference do you think it would make if Joshua was not careful to know and follow God's law?

How are obedience and success connected in Joshua 1:6–9?

God's message to Joshua in Joshua 1:2–9 can be divided into basically two parts. In verses 2–5, the Lord reaffirmed His promise to give the Israelites the land. To encourage Joshua, He finished with, "I will be with you. I will not leave you or forsake you" (Josh. 1:5). Then, after reminding Joshua of His promises, the Lord shifted His attention to His expectations of Joshua in verses 6–9. It can be tempting to limit our focus to the Lord's exhortation, "be strong and courageous" and "your God is with you wherever you go." After all, to "be strong and courageous" sounds inspiring on its own. I've quoted it a few times myself! And who doesn't want God to be "with you wherever you go"? However, when these passages are disconnected from a reverence for knowing and obeying God's Word, which is how we come to know God's heart, we open ourselves up for a distorted theology that will ultimately lead to all kinds of poor decisions.

To be truly effective (at least from a biblical view), being "strong and courageous" and having an assurance that "your God is with you wherever you go"[11] goes hand in hand with a healthy fear of God and a desire to obey His laws. Remember Shiphrah and Puah? The strength and courage of these two Hebrew midwives to stand up to Egypt's mighty Pharaoh is evidenced by the simple but profound fact that these women feared God (Exod. 1:17). We would be wise to not read those words too lightly.

However, obedience to God's laws is not a matter of legalistic perfectionism. Quite the opposite, in fact. It's a matter of the heart. Let's take a brief look at a passage in the book of Romans to help us keep these truths in their proper perspective.

Read the excerpt from Romans 4:13–16, which is printed below. Complete the passage by using the keywords (note: each keyword is used only once).

heirs   guaranteed   promise   Abraham   grace   faith   wrath

Bible study tip: When we disconnect passages from the surrounding context, we open ourselves up to a distorted theology that will ultimately lead to all kinds of poor decisions.

For the ______________ to Abraham and his offspring that he would be heir of the world did not come through the law but through the righteousness of ______________. For if it is the adherents of the law who are to be the ______________, faith is null and the promise is void. For the law brings ______________, but where there is no law there is no transgression. That is why it depends on faith, in order that the promise may rest on [or be according to] ______________ and be ______________ to all his offspring—not only to the adherent of the law but also to the one who shares the faith of ______________, who is the father of us all . . .

How many times does each of the following words appear in the text?

Faith ______________ Law ______________

Using your own words, briefly summarize the main point of the text in one or two sentences.

In Romans 7:7, the apostle Paul wrote, "Yet if it had not been for the law, I would not have known sin." Here Paul reminds us of the value of God's law: if it were not for God's law, we would not know what sin is. If we do not recognize our sin, we will not realize our desperate need for a Savior.[12]

Read Joshua 1:10-11 and 1:16-18. How did the people respond to Joshua's role as their new leader? Place an X on the line to indicate your response.

____

Vehemently opposed   Vehemently accepted

Explain.

The last verse of Joshua 1 packs quite a punch. The people not only embraced Joshua as their new leader, but they went so far as to vow that whoever disobeyed his words "shall be put to death" (Josh. 1:18). Wow, that's quite a commitment!

··YOUR TURN································

As a believer, what difference has it made to you to know that God will never leave you?

What fears might be keeping you from moving forward in your walk with God?

What one step can you take to bolster a healthy "fear of the LORD"? Write your commitment to God in a prayer.

Note: if you did not complete the last segment in the Pause to Ponder section on page 31 in Day Two, go back and do that now.

Lesson Summary

What scripture, statement, or thought was most significant to you this week? Write it down, and then reword it into a prayer of response to God.

One thing I love to do is end each week's lesson with a recommended worship song. You can find the full playlist at www.shadiahrichi.com/rahab (or simply www.rahabbiblestudy.com).

Notes

[1] For God to allow Adam and Eve to remain in the Garden would have resulted in the couple having continued access to the tree of life and, therefore, living in their fallen state while eternally separated from God. God loved His children too much, and so He provided another way. For a deeper exploration into the events of Genesis 3 and how they display the mercy of God, read "Week One: Reflecting on God's Risk" in my Bible study, *Legion: Rediscovering the God Who Rescues Me* (Abilene, TX: Leafwood Publishers, 2019).

[2] For a closer look at the fascinating events surrounding the worldwide flood, including a deeper exploration into the debated identity of the "sons of God" in Genesis 6, read "Week Three: Lessons from God's Flood" in my Bible study, *Tamar: Rediscovering the God Who Redeems Me* (Abilene, TX: Leafwood Publishers, 2021).

[3] Actually, his name was Abram at the time, and God later changed it to Abraham. To avoid confusion, I'm going to use Abraham throughout this study, except in Scripture quotations that use the older version of his name.

[4] A. W. Tozer, *The Knowledge of the Holy* (New York: HarperOne, 1961), 35.

[5] For a closer exploration into the story of Joseph and his brothers in Genesis 37, I encourage you to read my Bible study, *Tamar: Rediscovering the God Who Redeems Me*.

[6] David Noel Freedman, ed., "Egypt, History of," in *The Anchor Yale Bible Dictionary*, Logos Bible Software version (New York: Doubleday, 1992), 321.

[7] Stelman Smith and Judson Cornwall, *The Exhaustive Dictionary of Bible Names* (New Brunswick, NJ: Bridge-Logos, 1998), 223–24; emphasis mine.

[8] Smith and Cornwall, *Exhaustive Dictionary of Bible Names*, 198; emphasis mine.

[9] "Historical Books," in *Lexham Bible Dictionary*, ed. John D. Barry et al. (Bellingham, WA: Lexham Press, 2016).

[10] Douglas Mangum, "Joshua the General, Son of Nun," in *Lexham Bible Dictionary*.

[11] Of course, believers today are assured that the Holy Spirit of God dwells within us and will never depart (1 Cor. 3:16; 2 Tim. 1:14). Nevertheless, the passage in Joshua 1 serves as an important reminder that to trust and follow God depends, in part, on our commitment to strive to know Him by meditating on His Word, which is His self-revelation to us.

[12] Even so, no one will be able to stand before God and plead ignorance; see Romans 1:20, 2:15.

NOTES

PART II

THE
PROSTITUTE

HIDING IN THE ROCK OF SALVATION

THIS WEEK WE WILL MEET RAHAB, WHO LIVED IN THE city of Jericho—a thriving, militarily strategic city situated in a desert oasis in the land of Canaan. Today, Jericho is estimated to be the oldest inhabited city in the ancient world, with remains dating back more than ten thousand years.[1]

Jericho was also the first Canaanite city conquered by the Israelites in their quest to make the Promised Land their home.

DAY ONE
Born in a Wicked City

If you had asked me early in my Christian life to name some women in the Bible whom I considered to have exhibited strong faith, Rahab would not have made it on the list. First to enter my mind would probably have been Ruth from the Old Testament or Mary (mother of Jesus) from the New Testament.

How about you? Think of some women in the Bible whom you consider to have had a strong faith. On the following page and in no particular order, list the top three women who come to mind. Choose one, and next to her name, share something about her faith that stands out to you and why (optional: do this for all three).

The name Jericho means "a fragrant place."[3] The city was also commonly known as the "city of palm trees" (Deut. 34:3).

Interesting Fact: When the Bible was written, the Hebrew language had no word to designate a female god; as such, the Hebrews could only refer to them by their proper Canaanite names, such as *Asherah*.[4]

1.

2.

3.

God's Story: Part Two Begins

I like how the *ESV Study Bible* introduces the book of Joshua. It likens the book to "part two" of God's grand redemptive story. In part one, the Lord rescued His people out of slavery under the leadership of Moses. In part two, under Joshua's leadership, God brought His people into the Promised Land.[2] In part one, God gave His people His laws. In part two, He gave His people the land He promised to Abraham by covenant (Gen. 17:7–8). As it turned out, the first city on which Joshua set his sights was Jericho.

However, God's reasons for destroying the city of Jericho and others throughout the land of Canaan were not about punishing the inhabitants for sin. If it were, all the inhabitants of earth (including the Israelites!) deserved the same fate (Rom. 3:23). Rather, God's decision to single out the land of Canaan was His divine right. The psalmist reminds us, "The earth is the LORD's and the fullness thereof, the world and those who dwell therein" (Ps. 24:1; see also Job 41:11).

While the people of Canaan were indeed exceedingly evil, God's purpose in giving Joshua and the Israelites victory in their conquest of the land of Canaan was ultimately about carving out a place for God's name on earth (Deut. 12:1–5). God commanded His people to cleanse the land of unrepentant demon worshipers and their idols and altars to false gods because they were in the way of God using the land for His purposes.

While few historical records exist describing the religious life and customs of the people of Jericho specifically, there is plenty of evidence portraying the pagan religion and depraved lifestyle of the people of the land of Canaan in general. The Canaanite religion included various gods and goddesses who were primarily concerned with sex (fertility) and war. Worship of these counterfeit deities[5] (which were actually demons; see 1 Corinthians 10:20) involved a belief that if the gods and goddesses were pleased, the result would be victory in warfare, a thriving people, and a plentiful harvest.[6] To appease the gods, people engaged in human sacrifice (often children) and cult prostitution (both male and female temple prostitutes were common[7]).

These heinous practices were such an affront to God's holiness and such a violation of His purpose for human beings created in His image that God sent the Israelites to "vomit" the people out of the land (Lev. 18:25). Not only were the people acting wickedly, but the Israelites were at risk of joining in their perversions.

The People Rebel

The city of Shittim (a name meaning "acacia trees" in Hebrew) was the last place the Israelites camped before crossing the Jordan River into Canaan.

> Read Numbers 25:1–3. Fill in each verb describing the activities of the Israelites based on the passage. I completed the first one for you.
>
> [The Israelites] began to _whore_ with the daughters of Moab. These _____________ the people to the sacrifices of their gods, and the people _______ and _________ to their gods. So Israel ___________ himself to Baal of Peor.
>
> Glance back at the verbs you entered above. Where did the sin begin, and where did it eventually lead?

What conclusions can you draw? (Hint: see James 1:14–15)

What was God's response to the people's rebellion, according to Numbers 25:3?

PAUSE TO PONDER

Sometimes we think sin is a private matter. Perhaps you've heard it said (or thought it yourself): *As long as I am not hurting anyone else, why does it matter?* Have you found this assumption to be true in your own experience? Do you currently accept this assumption as true? Why or why not?

Having freed His beloved people from slavery in Egypt, imagine God's heartache and His brewing anger as He witnessed them turn away from His saving love—while camped on the edge of the Promised Land, no less! And to what did they turn? To pagan gods who exchanged dignity for shame, life for death, sacred for perverted—in a word: prostitution, both physically and spiritually.[8] Scripture teaches that, as a result, God's anger burned against His people (Num. 25:3). In fact, several Old Testament prophets would later cite Israel's failures at Shittim (specifically their worship of Baal-peor) in their efforts to warn God's people against falling back into idolatry and incurring God's wrath (Ps. 106:28; Hosea 9:10; Mic. 6:5).

Read Numbers 25:4–5. What did God instruct Moses to do?

The Lord's command to hang them in the sun "most likely refers to the ancient Near Eastern practice of impaling dead bodies on a stick after execution for heinous crimes, as a form of disgrace (rather than burying the bodies) and as a public warning to all who would be tempted to engage in such perversion themselves."[9] While none of us are in a position to pass judgment on God, that doesn't mean you and I will not struggle at times to understand God's actions.

What reason did God give for His demands? (Or to put it another way, what would God's instructions accomplish, according to Numbers 25:4?)

What was your first reaction when you read God's command in Numbers 25:4? Why do think you responded that way?

Interesting Fact: The only sins the Bible specifically reports as taking place in Canaan during the conquest to enter the Promised Land were committed by the Israelites (Num. 25:1–3).

Read Numbers 25:3–11 and 26:1–2. How many people died as a result of the plague that God sent in response to the people's idolatry?

What happened that ended the plague?

What specific reason is given for the Lord's commendation of Phinehas?

Why do you think being "jealous with [God's] jealousy" (that is, sharing God's zeal or holy wrath against His people's apostasy [Num. 25:11; see also 2 Corinthians 11:2]) is so important?

Upon entrance into the Promised Land with Joshua as their leader, Jericho would become the first Canaanite city destroyed by the Israelites.

Read Deuteronomy 18:9–13. List the offensive practices that the people were engaged in.

Based on the passage, all of the practices were "an abomination to the Lord" (Deut. 18:12). Look up the word *abomination* (or *abominable*) in a Bible dictionary, Bible encyclopedia, or standard dictionary. Rewrite the definition.

Next, read Deuteronomy 20:16–18. What reason is given for destroying the people who inhabited the land the Lord was giving to His people?

What does this reveal about God's heart for His people?

Consider God's desire to protect those who belong to Him from sinning against Him. What does this mean to you personally?

As finite and sinful creatures, there will be times when you and I may view God's commands as extreme or even harsh. However, God is more than ruler and judge; He is also our loving heavenly Father. As our Father, His commands are designed for our best interests and greatest good, whether we recognize it or not.

A Dangerous Path

I was fourteen years old the first time someone offered me illegal drugs. Having witnessed some of my family and friends engaging in the activity on several occasions, I accepted the offer. It began with marijuana, but alcohol and cocaine soon followed. My circle of friends began to change. More bad decisions, more destructive consequences, increasingly unhealthy relationships. Although I couldn't see it, I was heading down a dangerous path—and fast.

"Do not be deceived: 'Bad company ruins good morals.'" —1 Corinthians 15:33

PAUSE TO PONDER

Read 1 Corinthians 15:33 in the margin (optional: also read Galatians 6:1). Reflect on a time when you were tempted to imitate the behavior of "bad company." What was the outcome? How did it change you? Do you have any regrets? What did you learn?

Sometimes we think we are strong enough or smart enough to mingle with the wrong crowd without being influenced by their behaviors or beliefs. Sadly, most of human history, certainly as we trace the story of God's people in the Bible, proves otherwise. Yet, every so often, there are those who go against the crowd, who hold to their convictions, who believe that God is who He says He is. People like Joshua and Caleb, who risked being stoned to death for their efforts to convince their fellow Israelites that God would be faithful to fulfill His promise. Or Shiphrah and Puah, the Hebrew midwives who feared God more than the king of Egypt, knowing full well that their faith could cost them their lives.

And like the woman whose story we are about to see unfold: a prostitute living in the wicked city of Jericho. She did not personally witness God's miracles. She was not raised to know His laws. She merely heard about Israel's God—and believed.

································YOUR TURN································

If a friend came to you right now and asked what you are looking forward to the most from doing this Bible study, what would you say?

Explain your response; why is this important to you?

DAY TWO
Waiting for an Answer

Eight weeks ago, I received some difficult news. I had been living in my little rental home for the past eleven years when my landlord called. From the beginning, she and her brother (they both owned the home) knew of my efforts to serve God in ministry. For this and other reasons, they never raised the rent, which was truly a gift from the Lord. However, in our phone call, I was told that a decision had been made to sell the house—and quickly. I can't say that I blame them. Area property values are nearing an all-time high. Great news for them, but bad news for me because this also means that rents are soaring.

A Test of Faith

I've had difficulty sleeping these past few nights. *Where will I go? How will I afford it? Will the ministry suffer?* My mind tells me that God has a good plan for me, but the choice to trust Him with the details requires a deep level of faith—and I

"Search me, God, and know my heart; test me and know my anxious thoughts. See if there is any offensive way in me, and lead me in the way everlasting."
—Psalm 139:23–24 NIV

am struggling. Perhaps you've been there as well, or maybe you are experiencing a test of faith right now.

Waiting is hard. Ever since I received that phone call, my life has been in limbo as I wait for God to show me where I'll be living next. At the time I am writing these words, my deadline to move out is less than three weeks away, but I have yet to find an affordable solution. *God, are you there?*

PAUSE TO PONDER

Read Psalm 139:23–24 in the margin. Are there any anxious thoughts you are wrestling with today? Perhaps a difficult season where you struggle to see God's hand at work in your life? What would it look like for you to trust God in this situation? If you are not in a difficult season right now, take a few moments to praise God for carrying you through past trials and His faithfulness to carry you in the future.

During the first six weeks since receiving this unexpected and unwelcome news, I've been unable to write—not even in my journal. Yet, my mind has been cluttered with countless thoughts and questions. Maybe I have become too comfortable in my current home; could that be why God is moving me? Or maybe He wants to stretch my faith. Perhaps He has something wonderful planned—something better—but I can't see past my grief in leaving behind the gift God gave me in my current home.

In the meantime, the clock is ticking. Week after week, I look, I search, I pray, I cry, I reach out to friends in nearby churches—surely someone has an affordable solution. But week after week, God remains silent. Why? Have you ever experienced that? Asking God for direction, for answers, but all you hear is a faint—oh, so faint—*Wait*. For what? For how long? What do I do in the meantime? It's so hard to just wait.

I wonder if Rahab felt the same way, though clearly the stakes were infinitely higher—a matter of life and death! She knew the Israelite army was camped just on the other side of the Jordan River. She had heard of their victory over Egypt's Pharaoh and the other kings they had battled to reach this place. She also knew that even if she survived Israel's attack on Jericho, her life was about to drastically change. But when would it happen? And what would it look like? So many questions, but none that she could answer.

"Though you have not seen him, you love him. Though you do not now see him, you believe in him and rejoice with joy . . ."
—1 Peter 1:8

A Secret Mission

Read Joshua 2:1. Then, complete the table as follows. In the left column, list each person mentioned in the verse. In the middle column, describe what you know about them up to this point in the story. In the last column, record what they did (or how they were involved). I filled in two to get you started.

Person(s)	Who were they?	What did they do?
	Leader of Israelites	
Two men		

Optional: read all of chapter 13 in Numbers[10] as well as Numbers 14:1–10.

At the end of Day Four of last week, we briefly recounted the events recorded in Numbers 13 and the first part of Numbers 14—namely, that the report of ten fearful Israelite spies won out over the report of two faithful spies. Joshua and Caleb tried in vain to urge the people to believe in God's promise to give them the land. Instead, the people rejected their report, and God pronounced that they would spend the next forty years wandering in the wilderness until that entire faithless generation, save for Joshua and Caleb, died.

A Declaration of Faith

Keeping these events in your mind, glance back at Joshua 2:1. Why do you suppose Joshua sent the two spies secretly (that is, unbeknownst to the rest of the Israelite camp)?

Next, skip ahead a few verses and read Joshua 2:9–11. Then, answer the questions.

What was Rahab's first declaration? Fill in the missing words and phrases.

I _________ that the Lord has ___________ the land.

Next, record Rahab's last declaration by filling in the missing words and phrases.

. . . for the Lord your God, ___________ in the heavens above and on the earth beneath.

In the chart, compare and contrast Rahab's faith with the Israelites' faith a generation earlier. Next to each statement, circle either True or False. (Note: some responses call for speculation.)

Rahab		Israelites	
Saw miracles firsthand	True False	Saw miracles firsthand	True False
Only heard of miracles	True False	Only heard of miracles	True False
Desired freedom/rescue	True False	Desired freedom/rescue	True False
Considered it better to remain in prostitution (a form of slavery)	True False	Considered it better to remain in slavery *(hint: see Exodus 14:11–12)*	True False
Convinced God gave the Israelites the land	True False	Convinced God had given them the land *(hint: see Numbers 14:2–4)*	True False

What conclusions can you draw? (Hint: contrast the Israelites' background with what it may have been like for Rahab to be raised in the Canaanite religion.)

We will unpack these passages in more detail in the days ahead, but for now, they provide us with a beautiful glimpse into the mind and heart of Rahab. This will prove to be invaluable, because apart from her name and occupation, Scripture tells us little about her personal history.

Speaking of her name, I did a little research, as the meaning of a person's name in Scripture can sometimes shed light on the person or the events of his or her life. In the Bible, there are two spellings (versions) of the Hebrew name, which are both translated in English as "Rahab." One of these is used to represent a mythical sea creature (see Isaiah 51:9), as well as a poetic name for Egypt (not in a good way: see Psalm 87:4 and Isaiah 30:7). The meaning of the name in those and other similar passages is "fierce, insolent, or arrogant"[11] (or even "storm"[12]).

However, the name of Rahab, woman of Jericho, has a different meaning altogether. Her name in Hebrew means "spacious, broad, or wide place."[13] We do not want to read too much into the meaning of her name, but considering that God would one day weave Rahab's family line into the ancestry of the Savior of the world, perhaps "to widen" is a fitting name after all.

Over the next several weeks, we will dive into the depths of Rahab's story by unpacking the events slowly, verse by verse. However, before we do, I want to invite you to sit back, relax, and read through Rahab's story on your own. This will be your chance to take in the big picture. As this will require some extra reading, today's lesson is intentionally shortened to allow you the time needed to read through the passages.

...................................YOUR TURN...................................

Read Joshua 2 and 6, followed by Matthew 1:1–6 in the New Testament. Resist the temptation to rush. Savor the story. When you finish, answer the following questions:

Before starting this study, how familiar were you with Rahab's story? Place an X on the line to indicate your answer.

____

Not familiar   Very familiar

Did anything in today's reading surprise you? Explain.

Which part of Rahab's story intrigues you the most? Why?

DAY THREE
Sheltering Enemy Spies

Six weeks have gone by since I wrote yesterday's lesson. So much has happened in that small amount of time. One morning, after still not seeing an answer or hearing God's voice regarding my housing crisis, I finally picked up my journal and began to write. The words, which I share below, were nothing short of a plea of desperation. I didn't begin my prayer by acknowledging God's goodness or love, and I didn't remind Him that my deadline to move was just twelve days away. I didn't even pause to thank Him for hearing my prayer at all. I simply cried out, trusting that even though I couldn't see or hear Him, He was still near.

Father, I need You! I need You to fight for me. To open the door wide to the place You have for me. I need Your help. I need it now, Lord. I need You now.

I had reached the end of my rope.

I had nothing left. I needed God to fight for me. Near the end, I felt as if I was even fighting to hold on to my faith. Each morning, I felt confident in God's perfect plan for me, clinging to the truth of who He is—even speaking out loud the words from the book of Lamentations: "[Your mercies] are new every morning; great is your faithfulness" (Lam. 3:22–23). But when evening came and there was still no answer, I began to despair. I found myself crying out, "God, where are You? Have You forgotten me?" Well-meaning friends began to fuel my doubt by suggesting I was simply expecting too much: a quiet garden patio, a second bedroom for an office in a city where every square foot is at a premium. It seemed impossible. As the days passed by with no solution in sight, my heart struggled in the silence.

And then, just when I didn't think I could handle one more day, the phone rang. Little did I know that at the other end of town lived a dear widowed believer who had been praying for months that God would bring the right person to rent the lovely two-bedroom cottage behind her house. As she labored to plant colorful flowers that border the cottage's private patio, she asked God that even the flowers would be a blessing to the new tenant. Oh, how God answered that prayer! My beautiful new home is a gift from the Lord beyond anything I could have dreamed

or imagined. The owner is as much a gift as the cottage itself. Truly, her heart for the Lord and her faith in His perfect plan inspires me in my own walk with God.

PAUSE TO PONDER

Chances are that you have also experienced a time in your life when you felt you had reached the end of your rope. You knew the battle wasn't over, but you had no fight left in you. What did you do? Did you struggle with your faith? If so, how? If not, what helped you stay strong? In 2 Chronicles 20:15, we read that "the battle is not yours but God's." Do you suppose God allows us to experience these seasons to remind us of this truth? Explain.

A Different Mission

In yesterday's lesson, we learned in Joshua 2:1 that Israel's new leader sent two spies into the land, especially Jericho, to search it out. After their tragic rebellion, followed by forty years of wandering in the wilderness, God's people were on the verge of seeing the fulfillment of His promise to give them the land. God delivered them from slavery in Egypt, and He parted the Red Sea and drowned Pharaoh's army. He gave Moses and Joshua victory after victory over enemy kings. Just when they came to the edge of the river between them and the first city in their conquest to take the Promised Land, God put the whole drama on hold to tell us the story of Rahab. One commentary author explains that the Rahab story "appears to interrupt the logical connection between [Joshua] 1 and 3. The account's . . . location at the head of the conquest story, however, hints at its theological significance."[14] By the time you finish reading this study, I believe you'll never look at the story of Rahab the same way again.

Scripture could have simply recorded that the city of Jericho and its king were defeated. Instead, God dedicates more than a full chapter to tell us the story of Rahab. Have you ever wondered why God would give so much attention to a lone prostitute in a pagan city? After all, we already know that the spies' mission made no difference militarily. God's destruction of the city walls leading to the Israelites' victory would have taken place without any effort from the spies at all. Little did the spies know that God had them on a different mission altogether.

In Joshua 2, nine of the twenty-four verses (a little over one-third of the chapter) record Rahab's spoken words. To provide some perspective, I've listed below several prominent women in the Bible. Next to each one is the number of

Bible verses in which her spoken words appear. (Note: this list offers a general comparison, as the number of actual Hebrew words in any given verse varies.)

- Sarah, Abraham's wife: six verses
- Ruth (who has a whole book named after her): twelve verses
- Esther (another woman with an entire book named after her): eleven verses
- Woman at the well (the longest recorded one-on-one conversation between Jesus and another person; see John 4): nine verses
- Mary, mother of Jesus: fifteen verses, including the Magnificat, her song of praise in Luke 1:46–55

Based on these comparisons alone, it would seem that Rahab is in good company.

Read Joshua 2:1–5 (verse 1 is a review). After Joshua sent the spies out from their camp at Shittim, the writer immediately shifts our attention to the events that took place in Jericho. Next to each person(s) listed, briefly summarize what you know about them and/or what they did. I completed the first one for you.

Two spies: *Israelite men sent to spy in the land of Canaan, particularly Jericho*

Rahab:

Jericho informant(s):

King of Jericho:

Messengers sent to Rahab:

Consider all the people involved in the story as listed in the previous question. Throughout the chapter (even the entire book of Joshua), we are never told the names—except for one: Rahab.

Do you think this is significant? Why or why not?

We are only at the beginning of Rahab's story, and already we encounter mystery and intrigue. The Bible never tells us the names of the Israelite spies, nor the king of Jericho, or anyone else involved in the events surrounding the spies' mission at Jericho.[15] We are given just one name, and that of a prostitute, no less.

Both her name and profession have been remembered for all of human history since the day those events took place.

SUPPLEMENTAL READING

Was Rahab Really a Prostitute?

In the Bible, there are two Hebrew words that can be translated as *prostitute* in English. One is *zona*. This word refers to what we might describe as a street, or common, prostitute. The other word is *qadesh*, which refers to a temple (or shrine or cult) prostitute.[16] A simple examination of the biblical text leaves no doubt: the Hebrew word used to describe Rahab in the book of Joshua is *zona*.

Nevertheless, because Rahab is included in Christ's ancestry, church leaders in years past debated whether Rahab was indeed a prostitute. First-century historian and author Flavius Josephus chose to translate the description of Rahab's occupation in Joshua 2:1 to that of being an innkeeper.[17] Several others, including Adam Clarke, followed suit, preferring the less scandalous designation. Writings such as these, when coupled with the New Testament verse in Hebrews where Rahab is commended for welcoming the spies (Heb. 11:31), have led some scholars to suggest that Rahab was not an actual prostitute (even though the same verse, Hebrews 11:31, also mentions that Rahab had been a prostitute). (See also James 2:25.)

The idea that Rahab was merely an innkeeper[18] was likely prompted by a sincere desire to present the events surrounding the Savior's birth in the most favorable light. Unfortunately, while the motivation may have been admirable, these kinds of distortions fail to recognize and celebrate the heart of God's plan of salvation. The reality is that we are all sinners in need of a Savior. To anyone who has had even the smallest glimpse of the depths of the depravity of his or her own sin, the idea that God would choose a prostitute in a pagan city to become an ancestor to the Savior of the world is not something to conceal but to celebrate!

Spies Everywhere

After we read of the two spies entering Rahab's house, we learn that Jericho's king had informants at work as well. The Bible does not tell us how the Israelite spies entered the city. Did they sneak in at night? Did they walk through the city gate in broad daylight? Were they dressed in disguise? Whatever their tactic, they were quickly discovered. Maybe it was their accent, even though different languages and accents would have been commonplace in a large city situated so close to a strategic and vital river crossing.[19] Perhaps they were seen entering the city and were followed to Rahab's house. Or maybe it was Rahab's house that was being

> The idea that God would choose a prostitute in a pagan city to become an ancestor to the Savior of the world is not something to conceal but to celebrate!

watched. (Though it is not stated in the text, it would not be at all surprising if the king of Jericho even had ties to Rahab's "business.")

However the spies were discovered, in Joshua 2:2–3, we read that as soon as the king of Jericho learned that Israelite spies had arrived in the city and entered Rahab's house, he sent his men with a message to Rahab. In truth, these men, probably soldiers, were sent to capture the spies.

What did Rahab do, and how did she answer the king's messengers, according to Joshua 2:4–5?

What do you suppose the king would have done with the Israelite spies had Rahab complied with his command?

This was war, and nothing about war is pretty. Had the king been given his way, he likely would have tortured the Israelite spies before having them killed. Let's not forget Rahab's predicament. To disobey the king would have sealed her own demise, whether through torture, further sexual degradation, death, or all three. In short, to defy the king would have been a death sentence.

Describe one or two different choices Rahab could have made.

Consider the choice Rahab did make. Which words would you use to describe Rahab's character and actions based on what you know of her up to this point in the story? Circle as many as you like, or write your own in the space provided.

wise   foolish   cunning   daring   reckless

desperate   resilient   courageous

____

____

Explain your choices.

On the surface, Rahab seemed to have a lot going against her, especially in that time and culture. She was a woman, seemingly alone (her family was not living with her), who sold her body to survive. We are never told what led her to such a fate. Was she forced into prostitution to help pay off family debt (a sad but common occurrence)? Had she been married and then abandoned? Was she a young widow who turned to prostitution as her only means of survival? Did she envision selling herself was a ticket to a better life only to discover it would ravage her very soul? Whatever happened that led Rahab to become a prostitute, any attempt to glamorize her life or entertain the thought that she was content to stay that way would be a grave mistake. Even if Rahab was "her own boss" who set her own rules, no one grows up wanting to be enslaved to the sexual lusts of others.

Whatever her circumstances, when we get our first glimpse into Rahab's life, we already see hints of a woman with remarkable courage and resilience—a woman who recognized and seized upon a possible escape from her way of life; a woman who, despite all she may have had endured up to that point in her life, had not given up hope for her future.

··YOUR TURN···

Where in your life right now do you need your heavenly Father to fight for you?

Could God be calling you to take a courageous step of faith? If so, what might that look like?

Write a prayer of commitment as God leads you.

DAY FOUR
Taking Your First Steps of Faith

When we last read of Rahab, the Israelite spies were hidden on her roof while Rahab stood her ground at the door, weaving a convincing tale to throw off the king's messengers. To betray one's king and nation was a serious matter—this is still true today. But Rahab's actions and quick thinking revealed her as a wise and resourceful woman. Surely, she understood that even if her people could defeat the Israelites, she would still be trapped in a life that was, ultimately, a life of slavery.

Try to imagine what life might have been like for Rahab. List all the ways Rahab may have been in slavery—both literally and figuratively.

How appealing do you suppose a God who freed His people from slavery would have been from Rahab's perspective? Place an X on the line below to indicate your response.

____

Not appealing   Very appealing

Explain your response.

PAUSE TO PONDER

Where in your life have you faced a conflict whereby holding on to your faith pitted you against your family or community or even your nation? (A sobering example from world history is those who secretly protected Jewish citizens during the terror of the Holocaust during World War II.) In the end, what did you do? What did it cost you? Would you do things differently had you the chance to go back? What would you say to someone who is facing a similar situation?

Read Joshua 2:1–7 (verses 1–5 are review). List the four lies Rahab told the king's messengers, based on verses 4–5. I completed the first one for you.

1. *She did not know where the men were from.*

2.

3.

4.

What reason(s) did Rahab have for lying to the king, even at the risk of her life? Circle one.

Rahab feared God.

The Israelite spies were innocent men who had not done her (or anyone else) any harm.

Rahab recognized an opportunity to save herself (and her loved ones).

All of the above.

What do you suppose might have been Rahab's primary motivation for lying to the king? Explain your response. (Note: this question is designed for discussion purposes. As the response calls for speculation, there are no right or wrong answers.)

Now, think back to the story of the Hebrew midwives we explored last week. What reason(s) did the midwives have for lying to the king, even at the risk of their own lives? Circle one.

The midwives feared God.

The Hebrew boys were innocent.

The midwives recognized an opportunity to save themselves (from the king's wrath).

All of the above.

Glance back at Exodus 1:20–21. What appears to have been the midwives' primary motivation for lying to the king?

Interesting Fact: Flax is the oldest textile fiber known. It was used to make linen fabric for clothing.[20] Since flat roofs were ideal for drying the stalks, the mention of the flax suggests that Rahab may have made her own clothing or possibly engaged in selling fabric.

How did God choose to bless the midwives' decision to fear God above fearing the king?

Briefly skip ahead in your Bible and reread Joshua 6:25 and Matthew 1:5. How did God ultimately bless Rahab for her faith?

Compare and contrast God's blessings on the midwives and Rahab. In what ways did God's blessing on the Gentile prostitute surpass that of the Hebrew midwives?

Do you find God's lavish blessing on Rahab surprising? Encouraging? Puzzling?

Explain.

Despite God's blessing on Rahab, biblical scholars remain divided as to whether Rahab's willingness to lie should be praised, tolerated, or outright condemned. Some have even used the account as an opportunity to teach the virtue of honesty. However, the writers of the *ESV Study Bible* wisely remind us, "Given that [the book of Joshua] is a descriptive narrative, rather than prescriptive instruction, no general ethical principles can be drawn from [Rahab's] actions."[21]

In other words, the writer of the book of Joshua was simply providing a descriptive account of the events that took place. Because the narrative is not offering a lesson in honesty, virtue, warfare, or anything else, we would be wise not to try to force the text to find one. To do so is to risk missing the main thrust of the story and God's purpose for including it in His Holy Word.

Getting back to the story, based on Joshua 2:7, Rahab was successful in convincing the king's messengers that the spies had departed and that they should leave quickly to capture them. We can draw several presumptions from these events. First, Rahab appears to be a woman who could hold her own in the face of real danger. Whether this was an aspect of her character from birth or developed over time as a result of her dangerous occupation (or was a combination of both), we simply do not know. Either way, Rahab was prepared to go head-to-head with a group of imposing soldiers. That was risky. If the soldiers discovered the ruse, they would have brought Rahab to the king to be abused, tortured, or executed.

While Rahab's courage is certainly impressive, being brave is not always enough. Without wisdom, bravery can get a person killed. As it turns out, Rahab was also a woman who could think clearly and act quickly under pressure.

Consider her approach in answering the soldiers. First, she gained their trust by acknowledging that the spies did enter her house. Next, she downplayed her intelligence by feigning ignorance while simultaneously stroking the soldiers' egos, saying they would surely catch them. Then, for good measure, she weaved in a sense of urgency, deflecting the soldiers from pausing to second-guess whether she was telling the truth. This was brilliant!

But there was more to Rahab's character than confidence and cleverness. Rahab was also willing to risk her life to save the spies without any assurance she would be spared in the end. That took guts. Even if the spies agreed to the request she would soon propose, she had no guarantee they would keep their promise.

For us to see the driving force behind Rahab's courage to risk her life, we will finish today's lesson by taking a closer look at her confession of faith in Joshua 2:9–11, which we explored only briefly in Day Two.

Read Joshua 2:8–11. Then answer the questions.

Consider Rahab's first declaration in Joshua 2:9: "I know that the LORD has given you the land." Read the sentence slowly out loud three times, each time placing emphasis on one of the underlined phrases. Share one or two new insights or something that stands out to you.

Do you find the first declaration of Rahab's confession surprising? Intriguing? Hard to believe?

Explain.

> "For one will scarcely die for a righteous person—though perhaps for a good person one would dare even to die . . ."
>
> —Romans 5:7

In that time, the language of the Canaanites and other neighboring nations was not much different from Hebrew. This is evident by the fact that many names both of people and cities among the Canaanites were quite similar.[22]

For the Jewish people, God's name was considered so holy that it should never be spoken out loud. As such, the personal name God gave to Moses concerning Himself—"I AM WHO I AM" (Exod. 3:14)—is represented by the four Hebrew consonants, YHWH, which appear as "Lord" in the Old Testament.

There are several things about this first piece of Rahab's confession that are curious. First, although Joshua and the Israelites were still camped on the other side of the Jordan, here we read Rahab saying that "the Lord has given you the land." As in, it was done. Signed. Sealed. Delivered. In truth, Rahab's faith, as expressed in just this one short statement, could rival that of many of the Israelites.

To see it more clearly, we need to pause and consider the form of the verb being used. In English, Rahab's words are translated, "I know that the Lord has given you the land." While at the time Rahab was speaking the event had not happened yet, the verb is written in a form that denotes completion, which can be used for an event that happened previously or will happen in the future. It is the certainty of the event that is being conveyed. This is another clue into the sincerity of Rahab's faith.

Second, in the original Hebrew text, she called God by the name given to the Hebrew people: *Yahweh* (often translated "Lord" in English; see note in margin). She recognized God's special relationship with the Israelites and spoke of God as a person. Finally, the fact that she began her declaration with "I know" gives us (as it would have the spies) a strong indication of the depth of her faith. After all, we know that the spies were discovered on the same night they entered the city (Josh. 2:2). As such, Rahab had to act quickly, with no time to debate, waver, or doubt. This strongly suggests that Rahab's faith had been forming for some time prior to the night the spies entered her home.

In contrast, consider the generations of stories passed down among the Hebrew people and all that the Israelites had witnessed firsthand. To then encounter a woman living in a pagan land and raised in a wicked city who chose to risk her life solely on the reputation of an unseen God is to meet a woman of extraordinary faith.

YOUR TURN

Scripture teaches that God "desires all people to be saved and to come to the knowledge of the truth" (1 Tim. 2:4).

The Bible tells us that Jesus is the Son of God who came to earth to give His life to save sinners like you and me. Have you embraced God's gift of salvation through His Son Jesus Christ? If so, share the time and circumstances surrounding your experience. Follow it with a prayer of thanksgiving to God for His boundless love and faithfulness.

If you are unsure whether you have placed your faith in Jesus, why not respond right now by asking God to forgive your sins and commit to following Jesus as the Lord of your life from this day forward? Romans 10:9 promises, "If you confess with your mouth that Jesus is Lord and believe in your heart that God raised him from the dead, you will be saved."

If you prayed this prayer, write down your prayer with today's date. Then share your news with a friend, a group leader, or another member of the study. They will be thrilled!

DAY FIVE
Choosing a Different Path

At the end of yesterday's lesson, we began to unpack Rahab's profound confession of faith by looking at her first declaration: "I know that the LORD has given you the land." Today we will examine her full confession to see what else we can discover. Let's start by looking at the structure of the text.

A Remarkable Confession

In Scripture, we often come across a literary pattern called chiasm, whereby the writer intersects mirror images of words, concepts, or events to draw the reader's attention to a key event, central point, or something else that the writer wants to emphasize. To help readers see the pattern, biblical scholars typically use pairs of letters (such as A with A1, B with B1) to identify parallel words, phrases, or concepts when outlining a chiasm. Let's take a look at Rahab's confession of faith by outlining it in chiastic structure.

In the space below, I have outlined Joshua 2:9–11 in its chiastic structure. Fill in the blanks with the appropriate word or phrase based on the text. I completed one to get you started. (Note: Bible versions that adhere to a more literal translation, such as the English Standard Version, New American Standard Bible, or New King James Version, are best suited for this exercise.)

A   I know that the LORD has given you the land,

  B   and that the _fear_ of _______ has fallen upon us,

       and that all the inhabitants of the land melt away before you.

         C   For we have heard

                how the LORD dried up the water of the Red Sea . . .

                what you did to the two kings of the Amorites . . .

         C¹   As soon as we _______ it,

  B¹   our hearts <u>melted</u>,

       and there was no spirit [courage] left in any man because of _______,

A¹   for the _________, he is God in heavens above and on the earth beneath.

As you can see, the key words or concepts in lines A, B, and C are similar to those in A¹, B¹, and C¹, respectively. The writer's goal is to draw our attention to the point where the parallels intersect. Keeping that in mind, what are the key aspects of Rahab's confession, based on the chiastic structure you just completed? To put it another way: What was Rahab's faith anchored upon?

How about you? What is your faith anchored upon?

Rahab was not the only one who heard of God's power over nature and nations. She told the Israelite spies that every man in the city was in fear of them because of what they had heard. Yet, in the entire city of Jericho, there was only one person who responded in faith.

Of all the people living in the city, do you think it was a coincidence that the spies found themselves in Rahab's house?

Why or why not?

In 2 Timothy 2:19, we read that "The Lord knows those who are his." How do you see this principle at work in the story of Rahab up to this point?

PAUSE TO PONDER

When and how did you first hear about the God of the Bible? What was your initial response? Who was instrumental in your personal journey of faith, and in what way? Prayerfully reflect on the past month: Who has God brought into your life that needs to hear the good news of salvation? What examples of God's power or faithfulness could you share with them from your own life? (As an example, after God answered my prayers to provide the perfect rental home—including specific requests that, at the time, seemed close to impossible—many of my friends later remarked how God used my story to build their own faith.)

"But how can they call on him to save them unless they believe in him? And how can they believe in him if they have never heard about him? And how can they hear about him unless someone tells them?" —Romans 10:14 NLT

Following in the Footsteps of Faith

At the beginning of this week's lesson, I asked you to list the top three women in the Bible that come to mind who seem to exhibit a strong faith. Let's take a brief detour into the New Testament book of Hebrews, of which chapter 11 is often affectionately described as the Bible's "honor roll of faith," to see what we can discover.

Read all of Hebrews 11. List each woman the writer of Hebrews chose to single out by name.

Compare and contrast this list with your own. Any surprises? Disappointments? Encouragement? Share your thoughts.

I do not know about you, but on the surface, of all the women in the Bible the writer of Hebrews could have singled out, to include only Sarah and Rahab seems an odd choice. After all, Sarah initially struggled to believe God (don't we all?), and at one point even tried to circumvent His plan by using her servant Hagar to produce a child on her behalf.[23] And then, after the writer of Hebrews recounts numerous other stories, the only other woman mentioned by name who "made the list" is Rahab? Really? Let's see if we can find out why. Not only because we are curious (I certainly was), but also because the inclusion of Rahab in the book of Hebrews is going to be key in helping us put her story in its proper perspective as we near the end of our study.

It can be tempting to dive right into Joshua 2 and 6 and try to understand Rahab's story from within the boundaries of the chapters where her story appears. Some may go a bit further and take the time to examine the context of the entire book of Joshua itself, which is certainly a good start. But as careful students of the Bible, we can do better than that. For Rahab's story, even expanding our study by including an examination of the events in the Genesis and Exodus narratives that precede it, just as we have been doing, is still not enough. The story of Rahab goes beyond that. Simply put: Rahab's story is *big*.

I have a secret to share with you: Rahab's story is our story.

It's a story centered on three key themes, without which there would be no Bible, no gospel, and no Savior. Those themes are faith, grace, and salvation. The theological significance of Rahab's faith and its place in God's gracious plan of salvation is revealed by God's decision to include Rahab's story in key "faith" passages in both the Old and New Testaments. In addition to being listed in Matthew's account of Christ's ancestry, Rahab is mentioned in key New Testament passages—not once, but twice! We will examine those passages more closely in Week Six. For now, we will look at a few verses from Hebrews 11 and Deuteronomy 4, both of which will help guide us as we continue our deep dive into the beauty and significance of Rahab's story within God's overarching plan of salvation.

> Reread Hebrews 11:1-3, but this time, read the passage out loud. Compare and contrast these verses with Rahab's confession of faith in Joshua 2:9-11. What similarities can you discover?

Next, read the passage below, which is taken from Deuteronomy 4, where Moses was speaking to the people of Israel. They had recently defeated the kings of Sihon and Og (Deut. 2–3), and leadership would soon be transferred to Joshua, who would then lead them across the Jordan River to continue their conquest for the Promised Land.

> [The Lord your God] brought you out of Egypt with his own presence, by his great power, driving out before you nations greater and mightier than you, to bring you in, to give you their land for an inheritance, as it is this day, know therefore today, and lay it to your heart, that the Lord is God in heaven above and on the earth beneath; there is no other. (Deut. 4:37–39)

Look over the passage above, and draw a circle around every phrase that closely parallels key aspects of Rahab's confession of faith in Joshua 2:9–11.

Last, repeat the same exercise you did above for the passage printed below, taken directly from God's Ten Commandments as recorded by Moses:

> You shall have no other gods before me. You shall not make for yourself a carved image, or any likeness of anything that is in heaven above, or that is in the earth beneath, or that is in the water under the earth. (Exod. 20:3–4)

What conclusions can you draw?

In Deuteronomy 4, Moses could have referred to any number of miracles the people of Israel had experienced. He chose to remind them of two: God's deliverance from slavery in Egypt (which immediately brings to mind the parting of the Red Sea), and God giving His people victory over the powerful kings as they began to take over the Promised Land. On the surface, choosing these events makes perfect sense, as these would remind the people of God's power and deliverance.

However, the parallels we find in Rahab's confession of faith are striking, to say the least. For one thing, Rahab referred to the exact same two events mentioned by Moses for the basis of her faith. Next, she sandwiched these in between two dramatic declarations of who God is. The first is found in Joshua 2:9, where Rahab used the personal name *Yahweh* (represented in most English Bibles as "Lord"). Yahweh was the personal name that God gave to Moses directly (Exod. 3:14). Then, at the end of Rahab's confession in Joshua 2:11, Rahab declared that the God of the Israelites is "God in the heavens above and on the earth beneath." Almost everything in Rahab's confession mirrors Moses's exhortation to the people in Deuteronomy 4:37–39.

But that's not all. Rahab's declaration that Yahweh is "God in the heavens above and on the earth beneath" is also indirectly stated within the first and second of God's Ten Commandments (Exod. 20:3–4; Deut. 5:8). The phrase "in heaven above and on the earth beneath" (Deut. 4:39), as used in Deuteronomy 4:37–39 and the Ten Commandments and spoken by Rahab in Joshua 2:9–11, are the only times in the Old Testament where this phrase appears in the context of God's exclusive claim to sovereignty.[24]

Here we begin to get our first clear glimpse into the profound theological significance of Rahab's words, her faith, and her story's significance in the Bible as a whole.

And we are just getting started!

......................................YOUR TURN....................................

Before beginning this Bible study, how much significance would you have ascribed to the story of Rahab in the Bible? Place an X on the line to indicate your response. (Note: there is no right or wrong answer.)

____

Not very significant   Very significant

Explain your response.

At this point in the study, how much significance would you ascribe to the story of Rahab in the Bible? Place an X on the line to indicate your response.

____

Not very significant   Very significant

Are your responses different? Explain.

Consider what you have learned so far about Rahab's faith and choices. In what ways are you encouraged? In what ways are you challenged?

Lesson Summary

What scripture, statement, or thought was most significant to you this week? Write it down, and then reword it into a prayer of response to God.

There is a worship song for this week's lesson that I believe you will enjoy. Visit www. shadiahrichi.com/rahab (or www.rahabbiblestudy.com) to view the playlist. Once there, you will find other free resources as well.

Notes

[1] Walter A. Elwell and Barry J. Beitzel, "Jericho," in *Baker Encyclopedia of the Bible*, ed. Walter A. Elwell, vol. 2 (Grand Rapids: Baker Book House, 1988), 1119.

[2] *ESV Study Bible* (Wheaton, IL: Crossway, 2008), 389.

[3] Stelman Smith and Judson Cornwall, *The Exhaustive Dictionary of Bible Names* (New Brunswick, NJ: Bridge-Logos, 1998), 129.

[4] Walter A. Elwell and Barry J. Beitzel, "Canaanite Deities and Religion," in *Baker Encyclopedia of the Bible*, 413.

[5] In my Bible study, *Legion* (Abilene, TX: Leafwood Publishers, 2019), we examine the importance of recognizing that any "god" other than the one true living God is actually a demon.

[6] Elwell and Beitzel, "Canaanite Deities and Religion," 412.

[7] Elwell and Beitzel, "Canaanite Deities and Religion," 412.

[8] *ESV Study Bible*, 396.

[9] *ESV Study Bible*, 307.

[10] Numbers 13:33 mentions a people called the Nephilim (giants). For a brief but fascinating study into who the Nephilim might be, read "Week Three: Lessons from God's Flood" in my Bible study, *Tamar: Rediscovering the God Who Redeems Me* (Abilene, TX: Leafwood Publishers, 2021). The discoveries may surprise you!

[11] Smith and Cornwall, *Exhaustive Dictionary of Bible Names*, 201.

[12] Robert L. Thomas, *New American Standard Exhaustive Concordance, Updated Edition: Hebrew-Aramaic and Greek Dictionaries* (Anaheim: Foundation Publications, 1998).

[13] Smith and Cornwall, *Exhaustive Dictionary of Bible Names*, 201.

[14] Jerome F. D. Creach, "Joshua," in *Interpretation: A Bible Commentary for Teaching and Preaching* (Louisville, KY: Westminster John Knox Press, 2003), 31.

[15] Of course, we know the name of Joshua who sent the spies, but our focus here is on the events that took place in Jericho.

[16] In my Bible study *Tamar: Rediscovering the God Who Redeems Me*, I spend some time contrasting these two Hebrew words translated as "prostitute" in English, since both words appear in the fascinating story of Tamar and Judah, shedding additional light on the story.

[17] A. Edersheim, "Josephus (19)," in *A Dictionary of Christian Biography, Literature, Sects and Doctrines*, ed. William Smith and Henry Wace (London, UK: John Murray, 1877–87), 456.

[18] While Rahab's house may certainly have served as a lodging place for travelers (Josh. 2:1), her profession as a prostitute is clearly stated in Scripture (Josh. 2:1, 6:25; Heb. 11:31; James 2:25).

[19] Chris Hughes, *Rahab: Encountering the Woman Snatched from Destruction*, Face 2 Face series, ed. Simon J. Robinson (Leominster, UK: Day One, 2008), 6.

[20] Earl D. Radmacher, Ronald Barclay Allen, and H. Wayne House, *Nelson's New Illustrated Bible Commentary* (Nashville: Thomas Nelson, 1999), 276.

[21] *ESV Study Bible*, 396.

[22] N. Scott Amos and Timothy George, eds., *Joshua, Judges, Ruth*, Reformation Commentary on Scripture: Old Testament, vol. 4 (Downers Grove, IL: InterVarsity Press Academic, 2020), 37.

[23] For a fascinating exploration into the story of Hagar and God's beautiful plan for her life, I encourage you to read my Bible study, *Hagar: Rediscovering the God Who Sees Me* (Abilene, TX: Leafwood Publishers, 2017).

[24] As noted by John D. Barry et al., *Faithlife Study Bible*, Josh. 2:11 (Bellingham, WA: Lexham Press, 2012, 2016). (King Solomon used a somewhat similar wording in 1 Kings 8:23, but the emphasis was in a different context.)

NOTES

NOTES

CLINGING TO THE CORD OF
SALVATION

IMMEDIATELY AFTER RAHAB'S ASTOUNDING CONFESSION of faith, which we explored last week, we come to Rahab's negotiation with the spies. On the surface, we know the story: Rahab helped the spies escape, and, in turn, they promised to rescue her and her family when they took the city. But there was more going on here than meets the eye. Woven within the text of this critical exchange are each of the following:

- An oath
- A witness
- A sign
- Stipulations
- Sanctions

These embody the elements of a biblical covenant.

DAY ONE
Seeking God's Refuge

The *Lexham Bible Dictionary* classifies *covenant* into three types: kinship, treaty, or grant, depending upon which party swore the oath that ratified the covenant.[1] In a kinship covenant, both parties mutually pledged themselves to each other—often aiming for family reconciliation or creating new family-type bonds. In a treaty (or "vassal") covenant, the superior party imposed an oath upon the inferior (such as a stronger king requiring allegiance from a weaker king). A grant covenant occurred when a superior party bound itself to bless the inferior, typically as a reward for loyalty (an example is God's blessing on Abraham for Abraham's obedience in offering his son Isaac; see Genesis 22:15–18). As we are about to discover, the proposal Rahab presented to the spies reflected a kinship covenant.

Changing Sides

Read Joshua 2:8-14 (verses 8-11 are review). Now skip back one book in your Bible to the book of Deuteronomy. Read Deuteronomy 7:1-2, where Moses was speaking a message from the Lord to the Israelites. In the left column below, list each of God's instructions in Deuteronomy 7:2. In the right column, list each of Rahab's requests in Joshua 2:13-14. Be specific.

God's Instructions in Deuteronomy 7:2	Rahab's Requests in Joshua 2:13-14

"He fulfills the desire of those who fear him; he also hears their cry and saves them."

—Psalm 145:19

Compare and contrast the lists you completed. On a scale of 1 to 5, how well did Rahab's requests align with God's commands (1 being not aligned and 5 being fully aligned)? Place a circle around your response.

1   2   3   4   5

Consider your answer to the previous question. What was Rahab ultimately putting her hope in? (Hint: see Isaiah 56:6–7 and Psalm 145:19–20.)

You and I already know the outcome of the story: Rahab and her family would be saved from the coming destruction. On the surface, it seems that God's instructions and Rahab's requests (which were granted) contradicted each other.

When reading or studying the Bible, what steps do you take when you encounter passages that seem to contradict each other?

If you, like me, believe that the Bible is infallible (free from error), then the answer to reconcile such passages must also be found in the Bible. We might need to expand our reading of the book we are studying to gain a broader context, or we might need to examine other passages of the Bible that deal with the same topic.

In Deuteronomy 7:2, God warned the Israelites concerning the people groups they were about to dispossess (including the Canaanites): "you must *devote them to complete destruction*. You shall make *no covenant with them* and *show no mercy to them*" (emphasis mine). To reconcile God's command to destroy the Canaanites with God's willingness to spare a Canaanite prostitute and her family, we need to take a deeper dive into the reasons behind His command, as well as His view as to what made a person a Canaanite. The answer is found just three verses later.

As we briefly explored in Week Two, the Canaanite religion involved several heinous practices. I mentioned child sacrifice and cult prostitution, but all kinds of sexual depravity, sorcery, divination, and other vile behaviors were just as common. Keep this in mind as you work through the questions that follow.

Read Deuteronomy 7:2–5 (verse 2 is review). In addition to destroying the inhabitants, what did God require His people to do, according to verse 5? Be specific.

If you believe that the Bible is infallible, then the answer to reconcile seemingly contradictory passages must also be found in the Bible.

Interesting Fact: In Paul's admonition against practices "of the flesh" in contrast to "the Spirit" in Galatians 5:16–21, he mentions the improper use of drugs, or "sorcery" (also known as "magic arts"[2] or "witchcraft"[3]). The Greek word translated "sorcery" is *pharmakeia*—the basis for the English word *pharmacy*.

Why is this so important? (Hint: see Exodus 20:3-6.)

Read Exodus 22:20. Contrast Rahab's confession of faith in Joshua 2:9-11 with Exodus 22:20. (Hint: see also Deuteronomy 17:2-5.) In what ways could Rahab have

been called Canaanite?

not been considered Canaanite?

Explain.

How does Deuteronomy 7:3-5, together with Joshua 2:9-11, help explain why Rahab would not end up destroyed as God commanded?

What did God's protection of Rahab reveal about His character?

"For the LORD sees not as man sees: man looks on the outward appearance, but the LORD looks on the heart." —1 Samuel 16:7

While we must always guard ourselves against minimizing or disregarding God's commands, here we see an example where God led His two spies to recognize the faith of Rahab based on her words and actions. In light of God's command to destroy the inhabitants of Canaan and the assurance given to Rahab by the spies in Joshua 2:14, "we will deal kindly and faithfully with you," the writers of the *ESV Study Bible* offer this commentary:

This underscores the gracious character of the God of Israel and the fact that the boundary between Israel and Canaan was not drawn along ethnic lines but in terms of allegiance to the Lord. It also shows that there was room for exceptions in the general instruction to destroy the Canaanites, for people who came to genuine faith in the God of Israel.[4]

In other words, God does not judge people the same way we do. People often evaluate one another based on ethnicity, gender, social status, and myriad other factors, but God looks on one thing: the heart. Through the teaching of the New Testament, we see God's heart even more clearly. God hasn't changed, of course, but the Bible is a book of progressive revelation, and we are blessed to live in a time when God's written Word is complete and readily available to us. God's heart for all people and His promise to save all who belong to Him are beautifully expressed by the apostle Paul when he writes in Galatians, "There is neither Jew nor Greek, there is neither slave nor free, there is no male and female, for you are all one in Christ Jesus. And if you are Christ's, then you are Abraham's offspring, heirs according to promise" (Gal. 3:28–29).

God's heart for all people has never changed. We see this principle clearly at work even in the events we have been studying. At the time of God's command to destroy the Canaanites, the Israelite community included people from various other nations who had committed themselves to following the Lord. God revealed His heart for all people back in Genesis when He promised Abraham, "in you all the families of the earth shall be blessed" (Gen. 12:3). What a sweet picture of God's love and compassion, to welcome all who seek refuge in Him.

PAUSE TO PONDER

Read Deuteronomy 7:9. How has God proven Himself faithful to you this past week? If nothing specific comes to mind, pause to spend some time in prayer and ask God to show you. Read Revelation 5:9–10. Who do you wish to see included among this multitude of "ransomed" souls in heaven one day? What one specific step can you take this week to minister to one of those who comes to mind? Write a prayer of commitment in the margin or in a journal.

Fear versus Faith

All her life, Rahab had been surrounded by darkness. Whether she had heard of Israel's God since she was a child or her awareness of His reputation was recent, there was a point when Rahab responded in humble fear. Truly, it was God's gracious character to bless any who turn to Him that Rahab was banking on to save her. This is quite remarkable given the fact that Rahab likely knew little of the compassionate, personal aspects of God's nature—but that's part of the beauty of her story. She may have known very little about God, but God knew her.

Progressive revelation is the notion that God has revealed his truth and his redemptive plan in a progression from the Old Testament to the New Testament and that later revelation (such as the New Testament) builds on and adds to the truths about God that were known previously.[5]

God's great love and compassion compel Him to welcome all who seek refuge in Him.

"I the LORD search the heart and test the mind, to give every man according to his ways, according to the fruit of his deeds."

—Jeremiah 17:10

"To fear God and not be afraid—that is the paradox of faith."[6] —A. W. Tozer

God saw her reverent fear, her willingness to risk her life to protect two of His own, and her faith to believe that He would save her in the end.

Talk about faith! Even Rahab herself confessed that every person in the city was melting in fear of Israel's army and their God. And they should have. The reality is that every human heart should fear God—one day, everyone will stand before Him. But there is a fear of God that strikes terror in one's soul for the judgment that is coming and a fear of God that births faith leading to the joyous hope of salvation. It seems quite tragic that a lone Canaanite prostitute was the only person in the city who responded in faith. At the same time, how precious that God would see her, step in by sending the spies to her house, and deliver her from the coming judgment.

Listed below are a number of verses outlining many wonderful promises available to those who humbly "fear the LORD." Look up at least five verses, and write the letter that represents the verse next to its corresponding promise. I completed one for you.

Scripture Reference		Promise
A. Exodus 20:20	_____	Receive God's mercy
B. Psalm 25:12	_____	Refuge for your children
C. Psalm 25:14	_____	God takes pleasure in you
D. Psalm 145:19a	__H__	Wisdom
E. Psalm 145:19b	_____	Draws others to the Lord (multiplies)
F. Psalm 147:11	_____	Fulfills the desires [of your heart]
G. Proverbs 1:7	_____	Instruction on which way to go
H. Proverbs 9:10	_____	Friendship with the Lord
I. Proverbs 14:26	_____	Hears your cry and saves you
J. Proverbs 19:23	_____	Knowledge
K. Proverbs 28:14	_____	Keep you from sinning
L. Luke 1:50	_____	Finds life
M. Acts 9:31	_____	Blessed by the Lord

Complete the previous list for all the verses.

················· YOUR TURN ·······························

In the list, consider the various areas of your life right now. Place a check mark to the left of each area where you would say that you are generally being guided by "the fear of the LORD." Then, place a check mark to the right of each area where you have a tendency to operate out of your own strength and rely on your own decisions.

Guided by Fear of the Lord		Guided by Own Decisions
	Job/Career	
	Health	
	Parenting / Obeying Parents	
	Marriage/Relationships	
	School/Education	
	Finances	
	Home/Possessions	
	Ministry	
	Other:	

Look back at the list of promises available to those who "fear the LORD." Which promise do you need from God right now? Write the Bible verse that corresponds to the promise you need. If you did not identify the corresponding Bible verse for that particular promise, look up the promise keywords (such as *wisdom*, *refuge*, etc.) in a Bible concordance and write one or two Bible verses that speak to your need.

Reflect on the areas of your life that you identified as those where you tend to be guided by your own decisions. Bring each one to the Lord in prayer, and ask Him to show you one specific step you can make to begin to develop a healthy, humble "fear of the LORD." Write a prayer of commitment below; consider incorporating the words from Scripture that speak to your specific needs.

DAY TWO
Bargaining for Your Life

Rahab lived in an evil culture surrounded by evil nations. You and I can only imagine what she suffered in her lifetime up to this point. After repeatedly surrendering her body to the lusts of faceless, nameless men, how many times might she have laid alone in bed at night, wondering if there was anyone who truly loved her? Or if there was a god who cared about her? A god who didn't demand the slaughter of children or endless gifts or prayers that would never be answered? How many times might she have been tempted to become bitter, become callous, or spiral into despair?

We do not know the answers to these questions, but one thing we do know: there was a point—perhaps one night as she looked out her window into the night sky—when Rahab found herself drawn to a God she had heard about but had never seen; to the invisible One who created the stars, rules raging seas, and silences evil kings; to the God who frees His people from slavery and fights their battles; to the God who created heaven and earth; and perhaps, just maybe, a God who even cared to notice a lone prostitute gazing up at the stars, longing to be known.

The God of the Israelites was nothing like the gods with whom Rahab grew up: gods carved out of wood and stone, imposing but impotent, having faces that did not smile and mouths that did not speak. Because of these, her people had thrown their children in the fire, consulted with mediums and sorcerers, and committed all kinds of degrading sexual acts in the hopes of appeasing these so-called "gods." Apparently, the God whose name is Yahweh was not like anything Rahab had ever known. Now His army was coming to destroy her city as He destroyed the other wicked kingdoms.

Reflect on the country in which you are currently living. Would you describe your country's condition as the same, better, or worse as compared to the land of Canaan at the time God sent in the Israelites? Explain.

Whatever country you are currently living in, what aspects of your culture do you think God would find offensive today?

"And [the Lord] brought [Abraham] outside and said, 'Look toward heaven, and number the stars, if you are able to number them. . . . So shall your offspring be.'"

—Genesis 15:5

Consider the moral condition of our world today. If you were standing in God's place, how might you be tempted to respond?

Crying Out for Justice

I do not get angry easily, but there was one occasion I will never forget. As I was reading a news article, my heart began to pound wildly in my chest. It was a report about a large group of young women and girls taken captive in Africa and forced into sexual slavery. For months, I couldn't get the story out of my mind. I can't count how many times I cried out to God in prayer. As I pleaded with God to rescue the women, I couldn't help but also pray for two things. First, justice. I wanted those brutal kidnappers captured and locked away (to be honest, I wanted them dead). In my heart, I wrestled with wishing God would just wipe them off the face of the earth.

At the same time, I cried out for Christ's return to earth. I wanted to see an end to all evil. Numerous times, I prayed something like this: *Lord Jesus, come!! You see the evil! You know every soul suffering on this earth! What are You waiting for? Please, God, put an end to it all.*

PAUSE TO PONDER

Have you ever felt like that or prayed a similar prayer? I imagine most everyone who has lived in our broken world long enough reaches his or her limit of grief or anger over injustice—whether they believe in God or not. Think back on the last time you felt this way. Describe the circumstances. What helped you move past your grief or anger? What would you suggest to someone struggling over the injustice in our world today?

Again and again, I cried out to God against the injustice and suffering, and I begged Him to come back and put an end to it all. In truth, I knew in my heart these were just my emotions speaking, but they were real—and they were raw. Whenever I found myself struggling in this way, God would gently bring to my mind loved ones who do not yet know Him, including my mom and other family members who are still walking in darkness. I understood: one day soon it will be too late for those who are still living in rebellion, too late for all who refuse to step out of the darkness into the light (Rom. 2:8). As I thought about those who do not yet know Him, my heart would soften as God would bring to my mind a verse from the New Testament that reminds me of His blessed compassion—and patience—for the lost (2 Pet. 3:9). I would fall to my knees in gratitude, praising Him for His blessed patience with me.

Write 2 Peter 3:9 in the space below.

Look back a few verses to 2 Peter 3:4. Based on this verse, what is the "promise" that is being referred to in 2 Peter 3:9?

Finally, read 2 Peter 3:10, 3:13. What will happen when the Day of the Lord finally does come?

As Christians, why do you and I need not fear that day?

Rahab knew judgment was coming. She may not have understood everything—or much at all—about God's reasons for destroying the surrounding nations. But rather than shrinking back in fear, something within her spirit, which can only be explained as a gracious gift from God, compelled her to seek refuge in Him. One commentary writer explains, "Rahab might possibly have heard talk of God's promises made to his people to give them the country, but that she so firmly persuaded herself that it will come to pass proceeded from an internal work of God."[7]

PAUSE TO PONDER

Read Ephesians 2:8–9 in the margin (optional: read all of Ephesians 2:1–9). What first attracted you to the Lord? Did you hear stories of His deeds or testimonies from His people? A sermon? Did someone invite you to church? What led to you become a Christian? If you are not a Christian, what may be holding you back?

God's Steadfast Love Endures Forever

Read Joshua 2:12–13. When you read the word *kind* (or *kindly*), what comes to mind? How would you describe it?

Look up *kind* in a standard dictionary. Write the definition below.

"For by grace you have been saved through faith. And this is not your own doing; it is the gift of God, not a result of works, so that no one may boast."

—Ephesians 2:8–9

Despite the best efforts of skilled Bible translators, some of the force of this verbal transaction between Rahab and the spies can be lost in English. When you or I use the word *kind* (or *kindly*), we probably picture someone being considerate or courteous, but in ancient Hebrew, the word held far more weight. The word translated "kindly" in Joshua 2:12 and 14 is *chesed* in Hebrew, taken from the Hebrew root word *chasad*, meaning "to be good."

In ancient Near Eastern culture, to be good or kind (especially in the context of a covenant) was understood to mean that one would be loyal and faithful to the other person. Not only that, but in this case, the covenant between Rahab and the spies had no end date. It could be likened to the elements of traditional Christian marriage vows—a covenant in which the couple commit themselves to love, cherish, and remain faithful to one other "until death do us part."

God made a similar commitment when He described Himself as a "husband" to His people in Isaiah 54:5–10. Throughout the Old Testament, we read of God's steadfast (or loyal) love for His people. The word translated "steadfast love" is *hesed* in Hebrew and shares the same Hebrew root word used to translate "kindly" in Joshua 2.

References to God's steadfast love appear in numerous Old Testament passages, but none contain more occurrences of the expression than Psalm 136. Each of the psalm's twenty-six verses ends with a beautiful declaration that God's "steadfast love endures forever." Let's take a look at what stirred the psalmist's heart to praise God for His eternal steadfast love; but as we do, we'll also be looking at something else.

Psalm 136 is printed below. Before you read it, go back and reread Rahab's confession of faith in Joshua 2:9–11. Then, as you read through Psalm 136, place a circle around every phrase that is clearly reflected in Rahab's confession of faith (these phrases will likely be those that stand out right away). I circled one for you.

Next, underline every phrase that reflects concepts that are implied or indirectly reflected in Rahab's confession (these phrases may be less obvious). I underlined two for you.

Note: not everyone will complete this exercise in exactly the same way.

1 Give thanks to the LORD, for he is good,
   for his steadfast love endures forever.
2 Give thanks to the God of gods,
   for his steadfast love endures forever.
3 Give thanks to the Lord of lords,
   for his steadfast love endures forever;
4 to him who alone does great wonders,
   for his steadfast love endures forever;
5 to him who by understanding made the heavens,
   for his steadfast love endures forever;
6 to him who spread out the earth above the waters,
   for his steadfast love endures forever;
7 to him who made the great lights,
   for his steadfast love endures forever;
8 the sun to rule over the day,
   for his steadfast love endures forever;
9 the moon and stars to rule over the night,
   for his steadfast love endures forever;
10 to him who struck down the firstborn of Egypt,
   for his steadfast love endures forever;
11 and brought Israel out from among them,
   for his steadfast love endures forever;
12 with a strong hand and an outstretched arm,
   for his steadfast love endures forever;
13 to him who divided the Red Sea in two,

    for his steadfast love endures forever;
¹⁴ and made Israel pass through the midst of it,
    for his steadfast love endures forever;
¹⁵ but overthrew Pharaoh and his host in the Red Sea,
    for his steadfast love endures forever;
¹⁶ to him who led his people through the wilderness,
    for his steadfast love endures forever;
¹⁷ to him who struck down great kings,
    for his steadfast love endures forever;
¹⁸ and killed mighty kings,
    for his steadfast love endures forever;
¹⁹ Sihon, king of the Amorites,
    for his steadfast love endures forever;
²⁰ and Og, king of Bashan,
    for his steadfast love endures forever;
²¹ and gave their land as a heritage,
    for his steadfast love endures forever;
²² a heritage to Israel his servant,
    for his steadfast love endures forever.
²³ It is he who remembered us in our low estate,
    for his steadfast love endures forever;
²⁴ and rescued us from our foes,
    for his steadfast love endures forever;
²⁵ he who gives food to all flesh,
    for his steadfast love endures forever.
²⁶ Give thanks to the God of heaven,
    for his steadfast love endures forever.

Next to each phrase you underlined, write a brief explanation as to how it is reflected in Rahab's confession of faith. For example, Rahab's declaration in Joshua 2:11, "The Lord your God, he is God . . . ," reflects her conviction that God is "God of gods" and "Lord of lords" in Psalm 136:2–3, even if she didn't use those exact words.

After Rahab confessed her faith in God in Joshua 2:9–11, she asked the spies to swear an oath to "deal kindly" with her and her family. When we consider her request in the context of the deeper meaning of the word *kindly*, we realize that she was in effect asking for their perpetual loyalty. Just as she had forever forsaken her loyalty to her king and countrymen and turned to the God of the Israelites, the spies would now be obligated to protect Rahab and her family as if they were members of their own family.

The Old Testament is filled with sweet reminders of God's "steadfast love" (*hesed*). The expression appears in the Old Testament roughly two hundred times, with all but roughly twenty of these referring to the steadfast love of God.

Why does God's steadfast (loyal) love matter?

What does His steadfast love mean to you personally?

Optional Assignment: Write your own psalm-styled poem, celebrating the Lord for who He is, what He has done, or things He has promised. End each stanza with the phrase *for his steadfast (loyal) love endures forever*. The poem can be simply two or three lines or as long as you like. If you are doing this study with a group, consider sharing your poem.

DAY THREE
Stepping into the Light

Years ago, I worked as a property manager for Northern California's San Jose International Airport. High temperatures in this region average 75–80°F in the summer and 60–65°F in the winter. With more than three hundred days a year of sunshine, it boasts being one of the most pleasant places to live for those who enjoy a warm climate.

One morning, during our weekly management meeting, we learned that a new airline was planning to begin operations at the airport. Because the airline's home base was located in an exceptionally cold climate, when the local manager of the new airline arrived to begin setting up operations, he requested a copy of the airport's procedures for deicing an aircraft—a routine request at most every airport. Deicing is an essential safety process for removing snow, ice, or frost from an aircraft's surface, as ice buildup can weigh down the aircraft as well as hinder its ability to fly smoothly and safely.

Deicing procedures would typically include the type of chemicals or products used to dissolve the ice on the aircraft, the order of priority for the scheduled aircraft to take off if there were weather delays, steps required to prevent and clean up spills of hazardous materials, and so forth. This was a common request for any airline starting operations at a new airport. The following week, the local manager of the newly added airline was handed a sheet of paper outlining the procedures: "We park the aircraft in the Sun."

It was meant as a joke, and in truth, leaving the aircraft parked in the sun was sufficient most of the time at that airport, but it serves as a perfect illustration that sometimes we can make things too complicated.

This can be true even when sharing the good news of salvation. In keeping with the aircraft illustration, the gospel is essentially an invitation to recognize that we are hopelessly weighed down by sin. But God invites us to step into the purifying light of His love and rise up into the new life He desires for all who come to Him—not just one day in heaven, but here today. Right now.

PAUSE TO PONDER

Reflect on the last sentence in the paragraph above. Since becoming a Christian, how have you experienced "new life" right here on planet Earth? What changes have occurred in your life, relationships, outlook, and thoughts? How about now? How are you experiencing "new life" right now? If you are not yet a follower of Jesus, what may be standing in the way?

> "… the people dwelling in darkness have seen a great light, and for those dwelling in the region and shadow of death, on them a light has dawned."
>
> —Matthew 4:16

A Changed Life

Rahab's bold confession of faith and her courageous protection of the spies (at the risk of her own life!) are evidence that Rahab recognized and was drawn to the light of the one true God. After saving the spies from her murderous king, Rahab turned to the two men and got right to the point. Her proposal to the spies included the first three elements of a biblical covenant.

List the five key elements of a biblical covenant based on the list I provided at the beginning of this week's lesson.

Reread Joshua 2:12–14. Verse 12 is printed below. Underline the three keywords in verse 12 that represent the first three elements of the covenant. I underlined one of them for you.

> Now then, please swear to me by the LORD that, as I have dealt kindly with you, you also will deal kindly with my father's house, and give me a sure <u>sign</u>.

Next, in Joshua 2:13, after Rahab reminded the spies, "as I have dealt kindly with you," whom did she ask them to "deal kindly" with in return? Be specific.

What about Rahab's request stands out to you the most?

Why?

The expression "my father's house" in the Old Testament can refer to residences, inheritances, or tribes/clans.[8] Based on the context of Rahab's request, we can confidently rule out inheritance. That leaves us with either the residence of Rahab's father (meaning all those who lived in his home) or tribe/clan, which would include all family members belonging to the "father." To be certain which meaning is intended, we simply need to confirm that, as we might already presume, Rahab did not currently live in her "father's house." Though Scripture teaches us through words, there are other times when we can learn some things where Scripture is silent.

In the space next to each question below, write either True or False.

________ There is no mention of the presence or activity of any of Rahab's family members in Rahab's house.

_______ Rahab's house is described as the "house of a prostitute." (Hint: glance back at Joshua 2:1.)

_______ Skipping ahead briefly to Joshua 2:18, Rahab was instructed to gather (or bring in) her family (into her house).

Based on the above (all the answers are true), it would appear clear that Rahab was not living with her family. In fact, Rahab may have lived alone. Not only is no one else mentioned in the story, but Rahab did not request the protection of anyone other than her family. Besides, it would have been extremely difficult for someone living in the house not to notice Rahab talking with the soldiers at the door, hiding enemy spies on the roof, and negotiating her rescue. It appears that Rahab was all alone. Although she was separated from her family's home, she was not separated from them in her heart.

Rahab asked for the salvation of "her father's house." Her request would not only save her immediate family, but it would save future generations of her family line as well. After all, Rahab had no children of her own (if she had, surely she would have listed them in her request in Joshua 2:13). We can only wonder if Rahab had ever dreamed of having a different life, of having a husband who cherished her and children who filled her home with laughter—if she could even find such a husband in her wretched city or save any children she bore from being thrown into the fire.

But at least she could save the children that belonged to her brothers and sisters. Whatever led Rahab on the path to becoming a prostitute is anyone's guess. Her desire to preserve her family line would be fulfilled by God in a way she could never have imagined, but I'm getting ahead of myself.

My Father's House

Imagine you are Rahab presenting your request to the spies. Fill in the sentence with the first word(s) you might have said if you were in Rahab's place:

Now then, please swear to me by the LORD that, as I have dealt kindly with you, you also will deal kindly with _____________ .

What are the reasons you completed the sentence as you did?

While Rahab did include herself at the end of her request in verse 13 by adding "and deliver our lives from death," it is curious that she began with a plea to "deal

"The name of the LORD is a strong tower; the righteous man runs into it and is safe." —Proverbs 18:10

kindly with my father's house" (Josh. 2:12), which she specifically described as "my father and mother, my brothers and sisters, and all who belong to them" (Josh. 2:13).

But what about Rahab? Am I the only one who imagines that I would have begun my proposal with, "please swear to me . . . as I have dealt kindly with you, you also will deal kindly with *me* . . ."? Of course, I would beg that my family be included; I've been witnessing to them and praying for them over twenty-five years! At the time I am writing this, no one in my family shares my faith. Only my mom has shown some interest. She prayed once twenty years ago to accept God's gift of salvation through His Son Jesus, but apart from a handful of visits to church when I would visit her in New York, I have never seen any real change. To this day, I pray earnestly for her salvation and for the salvation of all my family.

I think it is beautiful how Rahab, rather than thinking of herself, thought of her family first. In that culture, family did not simply consist of one's relatives. The expression "father's house" often referred to one's entire tribe or clan. In other words, Rahab was asking that her family name not be destroyed forever.

Share three or four words or phrases you would use to describe Rahab's heart and character based on what you know of her up to this point in the story.

What aspects of her character stir your heart the most? Why?

You have certainly worked through a lot of material these past few days. Take a moment to give yourself a little break. Perhaps make a cup of coffee or tea. Stand up and do a few stretches. Or simply pause to take some long, deep breaths. Digging into the treasures of God's Word is deeply rewarding, but it can also be hard work. With that in mind, today's lesson is intentionally shortened to give you time to catch up if you need it. In fact, I think I'll take a break myself and go make a cup of my favorite tea.

························YOUR TURN························

Earlier in today's lesson, I shared a story that reminded me how we can sometimes make sharing the gospel too complicated.

Who first shared the good news with you? Did you respond immediately, or did you need more time?

Looking back, in what ways do you see God's grace at work in your life before you came to know Him personally?

Is there someone you have been struggling to share the good news with? Or perhaps there is someone you care about who has heard the gospel message but has yet to embrace God's gift of salvation. Ask the Lord how He might want you to extend grace to them as He continues to patiently draw them to Himself. Write a prayer as God leads.

Find my favorite tea and other fun facts at www.shadiahrichi.com/rahab.

DAY FOUR
God Is My Witness

We finished yesterday's lesson with Rahab presenting her request to the spies in Joshua 2:12. We noticed she thought of her family first. In another commentary on Joshua, the author remarks that Rahab's concern for her family "is in keeping with the thought patterns of the ancient Near East. It is also an indication of her unselfishness."[9] We see this same mindset continue into the first century with a strong admonition in 1 Timothy 5:8 (printed in the margin).

We also notice how Rahab used distinct covenant language in her request. We saw this yesterday where you underlined three keywords in Joshua 2:12. First, Rahab asked the spies to swear (that is, to make an oath) with her. In Old Testament times, a verbal oath was considered as binding as a written contract—the only obvious difference being the greater difficulty in proving an oath was made, unless there was a witness. The next thing Rahab did was invite a witness into the covenant:

"It is better to take refuge in the LORD than to trust in man."

—Psalm 118:8

"Swear to me by [Yahweh] . . ." This was one smart woman. After all, she could have simply said, "Swear to me . . ." and hoped the spies would keep their word.

However, Rahab didn't know these two men. Given Rahab's profession and whatever tragic choices or circumstances that led her there, chances are good that Rahab had far too many experiences with men who could not be trusted to keep their word. So she invited the Lord into the covenant.

Last, she asked for a "sure sign." This is the third element linked to covenant language. Since this sign is not revealed to the reader until verse 18, we will come back to that tomorrow.

In the meantime, Rahab presented her request to the spies, appealing to God's name (Yahweh) as a witness. But His role would be so much more. If the spies agreed, it would be Yahweh Himself who was responsible for ensuring that the spies kept their promise. This would have been no small matter to the Israelite spies. Whatever oath (or promise) they made "by the LORD" must be kept. Failing to do so would incur divine consequences. After all, God's name and reputation were at stake.

> Optional: for a perfect—and tragic—example, skip ahead and read Joshua 9. What did Joshua and the leaders fail to do, according to verse 14? What lessons can you glean from these events?

Shifting the Balance of Power

(Note: the following question is designed for discussion purposes. As the response calls for speculation, there are no right or wrong answers.) Please reread Joshua 2:12–13. Imagine you are Rahab and are presenting your proposal to the spies. In that moment:

What questions might be going through your mind?

What feelings might be stirring in your heart?

Consider all of the things that could have gone wrong for Rahab. List as many as you can think of.

Of the list you just made, which of these would concern you the most if you were standing in Rahab's sandals? Explain.

Regardless of how the men might respond to Rahab, she knew that she was ultimately at their mercy, as they were her only hope for rescue when the time came. We can only wonder what thoughts would be racing through her mind: *Can these men really be trusted? What if they kill me now that the soldiers are gone? Even if they spare my life, will they agree to my proposal? Will they keep their word? What if they leave and forget the promise they made? Will their God care enough to step in and save me?* Or maybe she dismissed such thoughts and stayed focused on her mission. Whatever was swirling around in Rahab's mind and heart in that moment, Rahab knew she was still vulnerable. At the same time, as long as the spies were hiding in Rahab's house, they did not exactly have the upper hand. After all, they were in enemy territory, everyone in the city was on edge, and the king of Jericho wanted them dead. On top of that, the city gate had been shut. In short, they were trapped.

But like the spies, Rahab was on a mission of her own. Moments earlier, she had successfully averted the king's soldiers with her quick thinking and wise words. Now she turned to the spies for her next move. Based on what happened next, the spies knew full well the precarious position they found themselves in.

Glance back at Joshua 2:14. Write the first promise the men made to Rahab, as recorded in the first sentence of the verse.

From a human standpoint, how would you assess the balance of power in this moment? Place an X on the line to indicate your response.

Rahab in power   Spies in power

Explain your response.

How ironic that two trained Israelite spies on a military mission found themselves at the mercy of a Canaanite prostitute. How like God to divinely orchestrate such an encounter. These are the kinds of stories that make studying the Bible so much fun. Surprising plot twists. Unassuming characters thrust onto center stage. Don't you just love how God uses the most unexpected people—those society might be content to shame or ignore—to reveal something beautiful about Himself?

PAUSE TO PONDER

How have you witnessed God using someone unexpected (maybe you) to reveal something about Himself or to accomplish His good purposes? Describe the circumstances. What might God have been aiming at? What was the outcome? Did you learn anything new about yourself? Did you learn anything new about God? Explain.

Had the spies not been fully convinced that God would give them success, their promise to Rahab would have been nothing short of a death wish. In effect, the spies were saying that if they failed to keep their word, rather than destroying Rahab along with the rest of the inhabitants of Jericho, God would strike them instead. These men would have been fully aware of God's command to destroy everyone in the city. But here is where we see God's grace at work. Despite the fact that Rahab was a Canaanite—and a prostitute no less—the spies recognized Rahab's new allegiance to God.

And for God, that was enough.

When Kindness Matters Most

In Joshua 2:14, the spies immediately agreed to Rahab's proposal with great intensity, saying, "Our life for yours even to death!" One commentary author describes their commitment as a blood oath.[10] This was a matter of life and death—for all three of them. The spies agreed to Rahab's request, but not before they introduced the next element of the covenant: a stipulation.

Refer once again to Joshua 2:14, and then answer the questions.

God often uses the most unexpected people to reveal something beautiful about Himself.

What stipulation (or condition) did the spies add to the agreement with Rahab?

In what ways would this stipulation protect both the spies *and* Rahab?

Spies:

Rahab:

With whom did the spies promise to "deal kindly and faithfully"? Be specific.

Compare and contrast the promise the spies made with Rahab's specific request in Joshua 2:12. How are they similar? How are they different?

Consider your answer to the last question. What significance might this have?

The spies were speaking with Rahab face-to-face. They had had no interaction with Rahab's family and had no knowledge of where her family members' loyalties lay. While they had agreed to Rahab's terms to save Rahab and her family, it is not so surprising that in their response, the focus shifted directly onto Rahab: "we will deal kindly and faithfully with *you*" (Josh. 2:14—emphasis mine).

An oath. A witness. A sign. Stipulations. . . .

Four of the five elements of a biblical covenant are included in the exchange between Rahab and the spies up to this point. There remained one last piece before the covenant was completed, which we will cover tomorrow. Until then, the writer of the book of Joshua offers us our first tiny hint into what Rahab's life may have been like.

Read Joshua 2:15. Where did Rahab live according to this verse? Be specific.

Just for fun, describe the mental picture that comes to your mind when you think of Rahab in her Jericho home. Do you imagine extravagance? Poverty? A house on a busy street? A quiet street? Did she live in a distinguished area of the city? Perhaps a seedy, dark corner?

Before sitting down to begin writing this Bible study, I had not given a lot of thought to where Rahab lived or what her living conditions might have been like. The existence of a window in the exterior city wall is common knowledge even among those only vaguely familiar with Rahab's story. But then I did some research and was surprised by what I discovered. I do not know what you picture in your mind when you think of Rahab's home. Without having much information, I simply imagined Rahab lived in a middle-class or perhaps lower middle-class home customary for her time and culture. But I was wrong.

Scripture tells us that Rahab's home was built "into the city wall, so that she lived in the wall" (Josh. 2:15). The city of Jericho was built up against the backside of a high mountain. Around the front and sides of the city was a double wall, which provided the city with a formidable defense. One commentary author informs us, "Archaeologists have discovered the space between such walls sometimes filled with rubble but at other times partitioned for storage or to provide dwelling space."[11] The writers of the *ESV Study Bible* explain that it was a "double wall structure, with houses of poorer individuals built between the inner and outer wall."[12] The city's double walls were its first direct line of offense against attack. As such, those living within (between) the walls were most vulnerable to invading armies. In contrast, the king of Jericho and more affluent citizens would have lived farther within the city.

Here, we have our first tangible glimpse into what Rahab's life may have been like. She lived in an area commonly occupied by the poor. A second hint is found in another small detail that we read earlier: the fact that Rahab had stalks of flax on her roof. Flax is the oldest textile fiber known. It was used to make linen fabric for clothing.[13] Flax could also be used as bedding or fodder for animals.[14] Maybe Rahab had rabbits or chickens. Or, since flat roofs were ideal for drying the stalks, the mention of the flax could mean that Rahab made her own clothes, an inevitable chore among those too poor to buy clothing.

Another possibility is that Rahab may have also engaged in the trade of producing and selling fabric to perhaps help her family, or to pay off family debt, or to try to improve her own quality of life. Based on clues we will come to further into the story, in all likelihood, Rahab used the flax to weave fabric, either for herself or others, or both.

While we cannot be entirely certain of every detail of Rahab's life, the fact that she lived in the city wall gives us a good indication that her life wasn't easy, as if being a prostitute in a violent and wicked city were not difficult enough.

··YOUR TURN································

Compare and contrast your initial idea of what Rahab's life may have been like with the few facts we have been able to glean from Scripture.

In what ways can you sympathize with Rahab?

In what ways are you encouraged by Rahab's story up to this point?

As you consider Rahab's life and the challenges she faced, does it give you a greater appreciation for God's blessings and protection in your life? If so, in what ways? Consider incorporating your gratitude for God's blessings into a prayer. Write your prayer below.

Day Five
Asking for a Sign

If there is one thing my friends know about me, it is the fact that I do not cook. It's not that I haven't tried, but I just never developed any real skill in that area. Since my brother graduated from the Culinary Institute of America and owns a popular restaurant in Upstate New York, I speculate that he alone snatched up all of the cooking genes my parents had to offer. As for me: zip. Nothing. I do like to bake a few things; I suppose that's something.

In case you're tempted to think I'm exaggerating about my lack of cooking skills, I'll share one story with you (trust me, I have others). My friend once gave me a wooden pizza paddle as a gift. I love pizza, but I had never owned a pizza paddle before. I wasted no time. During my next visit to the grocery store, I picked up a frozen pizza (that's about as close to cooking as I get; currently, I use my oven to store a mini toaster oven, but I digress).

I was eager to try it out. After preheating the oven, I carefully centered the frozen pizza on the paddle and popped it into the oven, setting the timer for thirty minutes. About fifteen minutes later, a curious smell began wafting into my home office. I got up to find the source of the smell and quickly found myself in the kitchen, where a small cloud of black smoke was filling the room. I opened the oven door to find both the pizza and the paddle on fire. I imagine you must be rolling your eyes about now, thinking, "Did you not realize the pizza paddle was made of *wood*?!" To answer your question, yes. But I assumed its purpose was to cook pizza. Maybe it was special wood. How was I supposed to know the paddle was only meant for removing the pizza from the oven after it was cooked?

After dousing everything with water, into the trash it went. I then picked up my phone and ordered a pizza.

A Virtuous Woman

Rahab, on the other hand, seemed to be quite industrious. She managed her own home, modest as it might have been. As mentioned earlier, the mention of the flax suggests she might have weaved fabric to make her clothing and/or to generate more income. If so, the reference to the scarlet cord later on could mean that she also dyed the fabrics she produced. One way or the other, it appears that Rahab was a hardworking woman. If we put Rahab's profession as a prostitute aside, Scripture would regard a woman such as her in high esteem.

Read Proverbs 31:10–31. Listed below are several activities and character traits describing the "excellent wife" of Proverbs 31. Place a circle around each one that is also true (or at least probable) of the prostitute Rahab. Note: as some answers call for speculation, not every person will answer this question in the same way. (Hint: flax was used to make linen.)

Trustworthy

Works with wool and/or flax

Hardworking

Cares for her family

Wise in business

Weaves/spins fabric

Generous to the poor

Clothed in scarlet

Husband is respected

Makes linen garments and sells them

Speaks with wisdom

Praised by her family

Fears the Lord

Consider the various parallels between Rahab and the woman described in Proverbs 31. Do you find them surprising? Does anything stand out to you? Share your thoughts.

Read verse 30 of Proverbs 31 in the margin. How might this principle reflect Rahab's experience?

"Charm is deceitful, and beauty is vain, but a woman who fears the Lord is to be praised." —Proverbs 31:30

Although Proverbs was not written until long after the book of Joshua, one commentator suggests that the parallels between Rahab and the ideal wife of

Proverbs 31 provide a helpful backdrop in understanding Rahab's story.[15] After all, the author of all Scripture is God Himself. Both women shared the timeless, godly virtues of hard work, wisdom, diligence, and caring for the needs of their family (recall Rahab putting her family first in her request to the spies in Joshua 2:12). Proverbs 31 also praises the woman for dressing her family in crimson and working with flax (verse 21). But most beautiful of all is its closing tribute: "a woman who fears the LORD is to be praised" (Prov. 31:30). Whether or not the parallels in Proverbs 31 hint at Rahab's future, one thing is for certain: Rahab was a woman who feared the Lord.

PAUSE TO PONDER

The "excellent woman" of Proverbs 31 has endured some debate. After all, who could live up to such a standard? However, when we step back and consider the passage metaphorically, we discover that the passage may also reflect God's ideal character for His church: Christ's bride. In other words, the character traits embodied in the passage are God's ideal for everyone who belongs to Him—whether male, female, married, or single—as we yield our lives to Him. With this broader understanding of the passage in mind, in what ways are you encouraged? In what ways do you fall short, and what steps can you take to improve?

A Thread of Hope

Although Rahab may have turned to Israel's God for help, she was not out of danger yet. Back at her house in the city of Jericho, there was still the matter of helping the spies escape. After all, her own life depended on it.

Using a Bible that adheres to a more literal translation (English Standard Version, New American Standard Bible, or New King James Version are recommended), read Joshua 2:15-22 to get an overview of the events (verse 15 is review). What did Rahab use to help the men escape from her window, according to verse 15?

Skip ahead briefly and look at verses 18 and 21. What did Rahab tie in her window after the spies departed from her home? Be specific.

What conclusions can you draw?

The word translated "rope" in Joshua 2:15 is *hebel* in Hebrew. In verses 18 and 21, the Hebrew word translated "cord" is *tiqwat*. From the start, we see a distinction being made between these two objects. But verse 18 gives us another clue. Verse 18 includes a second Hebrew word omitted in most English translations: *hut* (meaning "thread"). One commentator explains that the "two words together have the sense of a 'cord of thread.' . . . this seems to refer to a line not substantial enough to support the Israelite spies."[16] A helpful example is found in the story of Sampson and Delilah in Judges 16:12, which reads, "So Delilah took new ropes and bound him . . . But he snapped the ropes off his arms like a *thread*" (emphasis mine).

In Joshua 2:18, the Hebrew word *hut* (thread) is omitted in most English translations as being somewhat redundant, but when we examine the original text, the additional word helps us recognize that the rope in verse 15 was not one and the same with the scarlet cord Rahab tied in her window. Nothing in Scripture is random. The writer chose different words for a reason. The rope used to help the men escape would have needed to be strong and long (if the spies needed a rope in the first place, this reveals that Rahab's window would have been too high above the ground for the men to jump). But that solves only part of the problem. They would still need to quickly find a way to securely fasten the rope to something strong enough to hold each man as he climbed down the outside wall. Once the first spy reached the ground, it is highly unlikely that Rahab would have had the strength to bear the burden of the second man's full weight after the first one reached the ground. But there is another possibility.

Let's pause here for a moment and put on our detective hats: What purpose might a long rope, already securely fastened near the window and strong enough to support a man's weight, have had in Rahab's profession?

Interesting Fact: the Hebrew word translated "cord" in Joshua 2:18 is *tiqwah*, which has a second meaning, "to eagerly hope," as found in Ruth 1:12 and Psalm 62:5.

The Bible teaches that the enemy comes to steal and destroy (John 10:10), but God can take what the enemy uses against us and turn it around for something good (Gen. 50:20). How are these principles reflected in Rahab's story, particularly in how the rope may have been used in Rahab's profession before it was used to help the spies escape?

It is possible that the rope had been there all along. How convenient to have a means for men to come and go from Rahab's house without being seen.[17] If this was the case, what a wonderful picture of God taking something used for evil from Rahab's old life and turning it into something to serve His good purposes.

Next we come to the verbal exchange beginning in verse 16. The start of this verse can be translated "And she said" or "And she [had] said," in which case the conversation is a continuation from what is recorded previously. Once the men stepped outside Rahab's window to begin scaling the outer wall, they would be in no small hurry to climb down and escape the city. Some commentators suppose the conversation took place during their climb down, and others propose Rahab may have spoken to the men after they reached the ground. Another, more probable possibility is that the writer mentions the fact that the spies escaped from her window in verse 15 as a means of informing the reader that the negotiation for helping the spies escape was successful.

The writer then returns our attention to the rest of the conversation that took place prior to the spies climbing out of the window.

Reread Joshua 2:16 and 2:22 and then answer the questions.

List everything Rahab advised the spies to do.

To what extent did the spies follow Rahab's instructions?

Who appears to still have been in control based on these events?

Do you find this surprising? Encouraging? Perplexing? Share your thoughts.

Rahab had already proven herself trustworthy by hiding the spies and diverting the soldiers. Her earlier confession of faith did not merely consist of words, but also of action. Even more, she had shown herself to be wise and discerning, able to fool the king's men and convince the spies of the best course of action. Rather than directing the men down toward the Jordan Valley where the soldiers were undoubtedly looking for them, she advised them to go the opposite direction, up into the hills, and to wait there for three days. The men would be wise to follow her advice.

With their escape now in view, the men chose this moment to introduce a new stipulation to their agreement—in fact, they presented two. Previously, they agreed to Rahab's proposal on the condition that she keep their activity a secret. In truth, this would protect not only the spies, but Rahab and her family as well. But now they presented Rahab with two additional stipulations.

Reread Joshua 2:17–19 and answer the questions.

Write the two stipulations that the spies introduced to the agreement, according to verses 17–18.

1.

2.

Next, what sanctions were introduced to the agreement, according to verse 19?

Now the drama really begins to unfold. The men dodged the clutches of the king and were about to escape through a window in the city wall, but before they did, they instructed Rahab to tie a scarlet cord in the window when they came in to take the land. At last, we come to the "sure sign" Rahab asked for at the beginning (Josh. 2:12).

It was a sign that:

- from the spies' perspective, would make Rahab's home easy to identify.
- from Rahab's perspective, would ensure the safety of her and her family.
- from God's perspective, would forever identify Rahab as one of His own.

....YOUR TURN..

What difference has it made to you to be one of God's own?

Since becoming a Christian

In the past year

In the past week

How different might your life be today if you were not one of God's own?

Take a moment to reflect on the joys, privileges, and responsibilities of belonging to God. Record your thoughts.

If you have not yet embraced God's gift of salvation to become His beloved child, what may be holding you back?

Lesson Summary

What scripture, statement, or thought was most significant to you this week?
Write it down, and then reword it into a prayer of response to God.

In addition to the worship song playlist, I put together a beautiful scripture sheet, which you can download and print at www.shadiahrichi.com/rahab. I pray it blesses you!

Notes

[1] Scott Hahn, "Covenant," in *Lexham Bible Dictionary*, ed. John D. Barry et al. (Bellingham, WA: Lexham Press, 2016).

[2] Peter Barnes, *A Study Commentary on Galatians*, EP Study Commentary (Darlington, UK: Evangelical Press, 2006), 258.

[3] Donald K. Campbell, "Galatians," in *The Bible Knowledge Commentary: An Exposition of the Scriptures*, ed. J. F. Walvoord and R. B. Zuck, vol. 2 (Wheaton, IL: Victor Books, 1985), 607.

[4] *ESV Study Bible* (Wheaton, IL: Crossway, 2008), 396.

[5] Douglas Mangum, *Lexham Glossary of Theology* (Bellingham, WA: Lexham Press, 2014).

[6] A. W. Tozer, *The Knowledge of the Holy* (New York: HarperCollins, 1961), 84.

[7] N. Scott Amos and Timothy George, eds., *Joshua, Judges, Ruth,* Reformation Commentary on Scripture: Old Testament, vol. 4 (Downers Grove, IL: InterVarsity Press Academic, 2020), 36.

[8] "Father's House," in *Lexham Bible Dictionary*, 2016.

[9] Marten H. Woudstra, *The Book of Joshua*, The New International Commentary on the Old Testament (Grand Rapids: Eerdmans, 1981), 74.

[10] John D. Barry et al., *Faithlife Study Bible*, Josh. 2:14 (2012; reprint, Bellingham, WA: Lexham Press, 2016).

[11] Jerome F. D. Creach, "Joshua," in *Interpretation: A Bible Commentary for Teaching and Preaching* (Louisville, KY: Westminster John Knox Press, 2003), 34.

[12] *ESV Study Bible*, 397.

[13] Earl D. Radmacher, Ronald Barclay Allen, and H. Wayne House, *Nelson's New Illustrated Bible Commentary* (Nashville: Thomas Nelson), 276.

[14] Barry et al., *Faithlife Study Bible*, Josh. 2:6.

[15] Creach, "Joshua," 39.

[16] Creach, "Joshua," 38.

[17] Amos and George, eds., *Joshua, Judges, Ruth*, 43.

NOTES

PREPARING FOR THE DAY OF
SALVATION

AS RAHAB GATHERED HER FAMILY INTO THE SAFETY OF her home, the Lord prepared Joshua to take the city of Jericho—not with swords, but with shouts. After the earthshaking victory, the Israelites tasted the firstfruits of the Promised Land, while God smiled down from heaven on the first fruit of His spiritual harvest: a Canaanite prostitute named Rahab.

DAY ONE
Turning to the God of Salvation

In the Old Testament, once a kinship covenant was made, both parties would often share a meal to commemorate the event and reinforce the relationship. When we last read of Rahab, the spies had sworn by the Lord an oath to protect Rahab and her family. The spies then escaped the city by climbing down the outer wall using a rope from Rahab's window.

An oath. A witness. A sign. Stipulations. Sanctions. All five elements of a biblical covenant were in place. However, the custom of sharing a meal afterward is missing from the story. On the surface, this should not be surprising. After all, the spies would have been in no small hurry to get away. For the three of them to pause and sit down together for a meal would have been ludicrous. But the book of Joshua is not the end of Rahab's story—or ours.

> Reread Joshua 2:21. List the three actions by which we see evidence of Rahab's faith. I began the first one for you.
>
> 1.   *And she said,*
>
> 2.
>
> 3.

> Of the three actions you listed, which do you consider to be most courageous? Explain.

While Rahab is often remembered for the scarlet cord she tied in her window, her other actions of accepting the men's words on faith and letting them go (also on faith) took a lot of courage. (Not to mention her willingness to hide them in the first place, and even to lie to the king!) As the men climbed out the window, we can only imagine how tempting it might have been for her to ask them to take her with them right then and there. But rather than save her own skin, she again put herself at risk—this time by choosing to stay behind, to endure the battle that was to come, hoping beyond hope that she would survive, all to ensure that her family would be "saved alive" (Josh. 6:25).

Truly, this was a woman of extraordinary courage and resolve, an intriguing contrast to Jericho's king, army, and citizens, who were all melting in fear (Josh. 2:11). Rahab surely had her fears as well, but rather than being conquered by her fears, she allowed her "fear of the Lord" to direct her steps.

We can choose to be conquered by our fears, or we can allow our "fear of the Lord" to direct our steps.

PAUSE TO PONDER

What about Rahab's story up to this point do you find most encouraging or inspiring? As you consider Rahab's example of faith, in what ways, if any, is your own faith challenged? What one step will you take to develop the willingness to be a more faith-driven person?

IS GOD DIFFERENT IN THE OLD TESTAMENT THAN HE IS IN THE NEW TESTAMENT?

When someone reads or hears about the Bible, especially for the first time, he or she may be tempted to view God in the Old Testament as being angry and violent and the God in the New Testament, as revealed through the life of His Son, as kind and gentle.

However, a careful survey of both Testaments reveals that God never contradicts Himself. For example, in the Old Testament, some may be tempted to downplay God's mercy and grace, but then we read the story of King David, who committed adultery and murder. The law required that he be stoned to death, but because of David's humble repentance, God had mercy on him, though David's son died (2 Sam. 11–12). In the New Testament, some may be tempted to downplay God's holiness and justice, which requires He punish evil. But then we read in the book of Acts the story of Ananias and his wife Sapphira, who were both struck dead by God for lying (Acts 5). These are just two examples, but they help to remind us that God is the same yesterday, today, and tomorrow.

When we ponder God's wrath, we need to recognize it from a spiritual perspective and in the context of God's character, which is altogether perfect. God's wrath is never vindictive but rather an expression of His holy intolerance for evil. His wrath is in perfect harmony with His justice and righteousness and holiness. The greatest picture of God's love was expressed in His willingness to pour out His divine wrath on His Son as our substitute to spare us the eternal wrath our sins deserve. Romans 5:8 reminds us, "God shows his love for us in that while we were still sinners, Christ died for us."

All of Scripture is an unfolding story of who God is. The more the story unfolds, the more we see God reveal Himself as He relates to people. There is no place in all of history where God is less than who He is at any other moment

Bible study tip: We must know who God is as He has revealed Himself all through Scripture before we can teach about what He has done in any one part of Scripture.

in time (after all, God is outside time altogether). This is why whenever we teach any passage of Scripture, we must be mindful of the full redemptive story as revealed in all of Scripture. To teach apart from this overarching understanding will inevitably lead to error. We must know who God is as He has revealed Himself all through Scripture before we can teach about what He has done in any one part of Scripture.

God never changes. Just as we do not want to overemphasize God's holy wrath and judgment to the exclusion of his other attributes, we do not want to overemphasize His love and mercy, either. Whenever we lean to one extreme or the other, by minimizing or emphasizing one aspect of God's character over another, we distort our understanding of who God is—and when we do this, we commit idolatry: creating our own image of who God is.

If we focus too much on love and mercy, for example, we may neglect to teach others to nurture a healthy reverence for God's burning holiness, which cannot tolerate sin and evil. When we do this, we fail to deliver the gospel. Few people will be attracted to the message of God's love without first recognizing their need for God's forgiveness.

The psalmist laments, "there is no fear of God before his eyes" (Ps. 36:1). No fear of God. No fear of consequences. No fear of sin, hell, or Satan. The result is thinking they have no need of a Savior.

Give Me a Sign

In reverent fear (and faith!), Rahab tied the scarlet cord—the "sure sign" she asked for earlier—in her window.

The Hebrew word translated "sign" in Joshua 2:12 is *oth*. It is not unique in the Bible, as it occurs roughly one hundred times in the Old Testament. One-third of these appear together with the word "wonder," often referring to the miraculous "signs and wonders" performed by God. A number of other passages refer to miraculous signs performed by God's agents, such as Moses, who performed miraculous "signs" in the land of Egypt prior to the Exodus (Exod. 4–10).

The word appears in relation to the blood of the Passover lamb being a "sign" (or signal) on the Israelites' homes. We also find the word used in relation to the sign of a covenant God initiates (such as the rainbow in Genesis 9 or circumcision in Genesis 17). In short, although the word is somewhat common in the Bible, the events were anything but ordinary.

The use of the word in Joshua 2:12 is no exception. The *Lexham Analytical Lexicon of the Hebrew Bible* provides some helpful insights concerning the use of the Hebrew word *oth*. The lexicon divides the occurrences of the word into nine categories, with the majority of occurrences falling within two categories: miracles and signals. The occurrences of the word within both of these categories include an emphasis on conveying a message.[1] Two verses in this second category are of particular interest to our study. They are found in Exodus 12 and Joshua 2.

Read Exodus 12:3, 12:5–7, 12:12–13, and 12:21–23 and Joshua 2:9–13 and 2:18–21.

Listed in the table are various elements found in one or both of these stories. Place an X in the center column next to each if it appears in the story of the Exodus. In the last column, do the same for the story of Rahab. I completed the first row for you.

	Story of Exodus	Story of Rahab
Blood / color red	X	X
Sign		
Stay inside house		
Door/exit		
Imminent destruction of enemies		
Protection promised for those who take refuge in God		

Consider the stories you just explored. How are obedience and faith connected in the Exodus story?

Rahab's story?

What general principle can you glean from Rahab's story? Or, to put it another way, what can you learn from Rahab's example?

"For there is no distinction between Jew and [Gentile]; for the same Lord is Lord of all, bestowing his riches on all who call on him. For 'everyone who calls on the name of the Lord will be saved.'"

—Romans 10:12–13

A Scarlet Cord

Rahab had already confessed her belief in the Lord in Joshua 2:9–11. The simple act of placing the scarlet cord in her window was an outward sign of her internal faith. She may not have understood everything, but even here we see God's providence at work. The choice of a scarlet cord was not random. To Rahab, the cord may simply have been lying nearby. The spies may have viewed it exactly the same way, or perhaps God brought the story of the Exodus and the blood of the Passover lamb into their minds. Either way, the scarlet cord was God's doing. But this is not the first biblical story where a scarlet cord of thread appears in the Bible;[2] rather, it is the second. Not only are the events surrounding the first occurrence no less intriguing, but they will help provide surprising insights as we move forward in Rahab's story.

In my Bible study, *Tamar: Rediscovering the God Who Redeems Me*, we are introduced to Tamar, the Canaanite daughter-in-law of Judah, who is the first woman listed in the lineage of Christ. Being included—even named!—in Christ's lineage is quite an honor; one Rahab would share as well. But the circumstances that led Tamar to be woven into Christ's ancestry are curious to say the least.

To provide a little background: young Tamar was so desperate to be included in God's covenant family that she disguised herself as a prostitute (are you beginning to notice a theme?) and waited for her widowed father-in-law to pass by on the roadside. When Judah saw her, he immediately solicited her for sex, not knowing she was his daughter-in-law. God, who had prevented Tamar from conceiving earlier by Judah's wicked first-born and second-born sons, enabled Tamar to conceive by Judah not one son, but twins! If this union were not strange enough, the birth of the boys was even stranger.

Read Genesis 38:27–30. Write the name of each son next to the correct description.

______________ the twin with the scarlet thread on his hand

______________ the twin who came out first

The identification of the firstborn son was highly significant among the Israelites (as well as in Middle Eastern culture in general). We can only imagine how these events might have been a source of conflict between the brothers. In this case, the scarlet thread foreshadowed God's plan of salvation. Spiritually speaking, the scarlet thread points us to the redemption we have in Jesus, "the firstborn among many brothers" (Rom. 8:29), who shed His blood to save all who take refuge in Him (Matt. 26:28; Rom. 8:29; Heb. 12:23).

While neither the writer of Genesis nor the writer of Joshua had these images in mind (after all, Christ had not been born yet), God was weaving together a story far greater than the story of Tamar or Rahab, or even Moses or Joshua. Here we are given just a glimpse at what is coming. But we do not want to jump too far ahead, or we will miss the beauty of God's intimate care for one Canaanite prostitute. In truth, all the people of Jericho had an opportunity to be saved. Rahab herself said that the hearts of everyone in the city "melted" in fear and that "there was no spirit left in any man" (Josh. 2:11). They all recognized God's power. The only difference was that Rahab turned to the Lord, and the others did not.

······················ YOUR TURN ······························

If at any time I declare concerning a nation or a kingdom, that I
will pluck up and break down and destroy it, and if that nation,
concerning which I have spoken, turns from its evil, I will relent of the
disaster that I intended to do to it.

—Jeremiah 18:7–8

Read Jeremiah 18:7–8 printed above. What does this passage reveal about God's heart for all nations?

But if a wicked person turns away from all his sins that he has committed
and keeps all my statutes and does what is just and right,
he shall surely live; he shall not die.

—Ezekiel 18:21

Read Ezekiel 18:21 printed above. What does this passage reveal about God's heart for each person individually?

What do these truths, along with Isaiah 45:22 in the margin, mean to you personally?

DAY TWO
Trusting in God's Faithfulness

"Ha! We took bets on whether you could color outside the lines—the resounding answer was *no*."

That was my friend's comment several years ago. I had the flu, and my Bible study group kindly brought me groceries (actually, they left the bag on the porch, rang the doorbell, and took off—not that I blamed them). However, to my surprise, at the bottom of the bag was a coloring book and crayons. I laughed at first, but by that time, I had been stuck in the house for over a week. When I shared a drawing on social media, my friends teased me, "We knew you would never color outside the lines!" In my defense, I did draw a cross in the back of the ballroom. I decided it was time for the princess to meet Jesus.

Truly, I love my Bible study group. They know me too well. When I was writing my Bible study *Hagar*, they patiently listened to my frustrations.

"I just can't seem to finish Chapter Five."

"Why don't you just start working on Chapter Six?" someone asked.

"Because I want to finish Chapter Five."

I like things to be done in order. Just as I do not like to color outside the lines, it seemed wrong to write Chapter Six before I finished Chapter Five. Yet, my friends gently challenged me, "What if God has a different order in mind?"

PAUSE TO PONDER

Where in your life right now are you feeling frustrated and unable to move forward? Perhaps having assumptions of how things are supposed to be done, or when or in what order. Inevitably, all of us find ourselves trapped in a box of our own making at one time or another. What if you were to step outside your current situation and ask yourself, "What if God has a different _________ in mind?" Choose a word, such as *plan*, *order*, *schedule*, or *goal*, and complete the last sentence. Then, spend some time with God in prayer, and ask Him to show you what He might have in mind for you concerning your present situation.

An Interruption

In the book of Joshua, particularly surrounding the story of Rahab, there are various references to a period of "three days." Because it is not immediately clear if these are separate or the same periods, the timeline might seem confusing. When reading narrative (story) passages in the Bible, there are times, like this one, when events can seem to overlap or be out of order. When we read a story, we naturally picture the events in our minds happening chronologically. But that is not always how the events are written. When this happens in the Bible, a careful examination of other passages can often help shed some light as we work to reconstruct the timeline. We do this for good reason, because the timeline will provide even further insights into the events.

Read Joshua 2:22–24 and 3:1–2.

Within this passage, we come across the third and fourth mention of "three days" in the book of Joshua. Commentators have wrestled with how to reconcile the "three days" in Joshua 1:11 with the "three days" mentioned in Joshua 3:2. Adding to the timeline confusion, Rahab instructed the two spies to hide for three days (Josh. 2:16), and they followed her advice (Josh. 2:22). Without spending too much time on this, there are essentially three possibilities.

One possibility is that all of the occurrences represent separate periods, amounting to a total of nine days. However, this places Joshua's announcement in chapter 1 in question; hence, many reject this view. Another possibility is that the three days in chapters 1 and 3 are the same, with chapter 3 simply picking up where chapter 1 left off. If that is the case, we are left with two possibilities. The three days in chapters 1 and 3 took place after the spies returned, in which case the Israelites would have crossed the Jordan into the Promised Land on the seventh day (see Joshua 3:5).[3] Or, Joshua sent the spies prior to giving the command to cross the Jordan in chapter 1[4] (Joshua 2:1 can also be translated, "And Joshua . . . [had] sent two men . . ."), in which case the three days in chapter 2 are concurrent with the three days in chapters 2 and 3.

To help shed some light on the matter, we will put a placeholder in the book of Joshua and briefly step back—all the way back to the beginning, to the first "third day" in creation.

> Read Genesis 1:9–13. On which day of creation week did these events take place?

> Read Joshua 3:1–3, 3:7 (verses 1–2 are review). How many days had passed after the people arrived at the Jordan River when Joshua gave the command to cross?

God's creation of the world was perfect. A true paradise. Although He knew Adam and Eve would ultimately reject His authority, resulting in sin polluting His beautiful creation, the longing for paradise still echoes in every human heart. The entrance into the Promised Land is a foreshadow of the eternal paradise God is preparing for all who belong to Him.

> Compare Genesis 1:9 with Joshua 3:16–17. Note the similarities by completing the passages based on the text.

> Let the ______________ under the heavens be ______________ together into one place, and let the ________________ appear. (Gen. 1:9)

> the ______________ coming down from above stood and rose up in a ____________ very far away . . . and all Israel was passing over on ______________ until all the nation finished passing over the Jordan. (Josh. 3:16–17)

It is no coincidence that when Joshua led God's people across the Jordan to take the Promised Land on the third day, we are reminded of God's activity on the third day of creation. If this is the case, then crossing into the Promised Land on the seventh day completed the connection. It reminds us of the seventh day of creation week—a holy day of rest and sweet communion with God—and it serves as a foreshadow of a greater rest that awaits all who belong to Him (Heb. 4:8–10).

However, perhaps even more striking is the fact that in between Joshua's command to cross the Jordan in chapter 1 and the people crossing in chapter 3, God put the entire drama on hold.

"So then, there remains a Sabbath rest for the people of God . . ."

—Hebrews 4:9

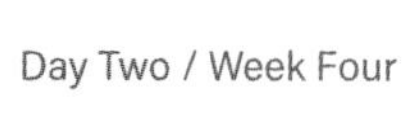

Mind you, this was the entrance into the Promised Land! This was the event God's people had been waiting for and dreaming of for hundreds of years. It was the event that would transform a wandering desert tribe into God's nation on earth. What could be so important that God would bring His people to the edge, only to put the entire event on hold? The answer? To save the life of a lone prostitute who humbly feared the Lord. Jesus Himself tells us in Luke 15:10, "there is joy before the angels of God over one sinner who repents." Rahab's life was no less precious to God than His entire covenant nation. What we might be tempted to view as an interruption was nothing short of God's divine intervention.[5]

An Intervention

Just as God rescued Noah and his family from judgment in the flood, as well as Lot and his family from the incineration of wicked Sodom, here we see God's mercy in delivering Rahab and her family from the coming destruction of the condemned city of Jericho. Nevertheless, although Rahab possessed a healthy and humble "fear of the LORD," convincing everyone in her family to take refuge in her house may not necessarily have been an easy task.

> Try to imagine being in Rahab's sandals, facing your family with the news that they needed to immediately take refuge in your house. What are some of the challenges and risks you might be faced with? (Note: as this question calls for speculation, there are no right or wrong answers.) I shared two to get you started.

Challenges	Risks
Will they believe my story?	*Will they betray me to the king?*

What we might view as an interruption was nothing short of God's divine intervention.

Of the lists you made, which challenge or risk would you personally find most difficult?

Why? ⟳

"…this is the one to whom I will look: he who is humble and contrite in spirit and trembles at my word."

—Isaiah 66:2

Nothing about this could have been easy for Rahab. What if someone in her family betrayed her secret, perhaps thinking they could exchange the information for the king's protection? Maybe there were past hurts or betrayals Rahab needed to forgive (or at least put aside). Yet, an army invasion was coming, and the whole city was in fear of the God of the Israelites. Perhaps convincing her family to take refuge with her was easier than she expected. After all, what did they have to lose?

Scripture teaches that God takes no pleasure in the death of anyone (Ezek. 18:32). In keeping with His character, God's desire was to extend mercy to any Canaanite who humbly feared Him as Rahab had done, evidenced by her willingness to show kindness to God's people, even at the risk of her life. We find this truth written in the book of Joshua itself, just several chapters later. Let's skip ahead briefly and take a look.

Joshua 11 summarizes the Israelites' conquests in northern Canaan (of which Jericho was a part). Write Joshua 11:19 below.

Since Jericho was part of the region referenced, what conclusions can you draw?

These kinds of passages—the rescue of a Canaanite prostitute, the opportunity for the Canaanite kings to make peace with the people of Israel—help us put God's command to destroy the inhabitants of the land in perspective. God is holy and cannot tolerate wickedness. At the same time, He never turns away anyone who comes to Him in reverent fear and humble faith, no matter how small or ill-informed his or her faith may be. The fact that Joshua 11:19 tells us, "There was not a city that made peace with the people of Israel except the . . . inhabitants of Gibeon" implies that "all the Canaanites were given opportunity to make peace, but they refused."[6]

An Encouraging Report

Reread Joshua 2:24 and then answer the questions.

What new information did the spies give to Joshua?

How was the faith of the spies revealed in their report?

Imagine you are Joshua. What kind of information would you be expecting or hoping for from the spies?

Exodus 15:15–16, printed below, is taken from the song that Moses and the Israelites sang to the Lord after He delivered them from Egypt by parting the Red Sea. Compare this passage with the spies' report in Joshua 2:24. Underline the similarities.

> Now are the chiefs of Edom dismayed;
> > trembling seizes the leaders of Moab;
> > all the inhabitants of Canaan have melted away.
> Terror and dread fall upon them;
> > because of the greatness of your arm, they are still as a stone,
> till your people, O Lord, pass by,
> > till the people pass by whom you have purchased.

Moses never stepped foot in the Promised Land, yet included in this powerful song of deliverance (Exod. 15:1–18) is a prophecy regarding victory over the land of Canaan. Without a doubt, the Israelites would have sung this song many times as a reminder of God's promise. Even more, singing God's Word is a powerful method for impressing God's Word into one's mind and heart. Joshua, having been Moses's assistant and eventual successor, would have been familiar with the song.

Imagine that you are Joshua, Israel's leader, preparing to destroy the Canaanite nations. How do you suppose he may have reacted upon hearing of God's words coming straight out of a Canaanite prostitute's mouth?

Explain.

Joshua was wise in choosing his two spies. They carried out their mission and were even willing to put their lives at risk, and, unlike the ten spies one generation earlier, they returned to their leader with an encouraging report. However, of all the things Joshua may have hoped to learn from the spies, such as a breach in the city wall or information about Jericho's army, the words of Moses's song, "all the inhabitants of Canaan have melted away," may have been furthest from his mind. Yet, these words, which the spies delivered almost verbatim as Rahab spoke to them, were the only new thing the spies had to report.

Reflect once more on Joshua 2:24. Despite the lack of helpful strategic or military information, how might the spies' report have encouraged

Joshua?

the Israelites?

God knows our weaknesses, but rather than shaming us, He gently reassures us.

One commentary author writes, "Although the mere promise of possessing the land ought to have been sufficient, yet the Lord is so very indulgent to [the people's] weakness that, for the sake of removing all doubt, he confirms [by the spies' report] what he had promised."[7] Another notes, "God used [the spies'] mission to reward Rahab's faith and reassure the Israelites."[8]

What a gentle, compassionate God we serve! He knows our weaknesses, and rather than shaming His people, He reassures us.

Who was the first person (or the person who stands out most in your memory) with whom you shared the message of the gospel, and how did they respond?

What motivated you or gave you the courage to share the gospel with this person?

When was the last time you shared the gospel with someone, and how did they respond?

If you have not recently shared the gospel with anyone, reflect on what motivated you the first time; has anything changed?

Consider the reality of Christ's imminent return and the implications for those who do not know Him. If you could change one thing within your own heart or mind, what would it be? Give your request to God through prayer. Write your prayer below or in your journal.

Day Three
Taking Refuge in God's Mercy

Finally, after four hundred years of waiting, the time for the Israelites to take the Promised Land had come. We are not going to cover all the details, but before we dive into Joshua 6, where Rahab reenters the story and the famous walls of Jericho fall, there are a few key events in chapters 3–5 that we do not want to miss, as they provide important context for what we are studying.

> Read Joshua 3:5-8, 3:13, 3:17 and 4:1-7, 4:14-18, and 4:23-24 (optional: read all of Joshua 3 and 4). Following is a brief overview of several key events. Using the keywords, complete the sentences by filling in the missing words.
>
> know   consecrate   memorial   priests   tribe   exalt   covenant
>
> The people were commanded to ______________ themselves (that is, to spiritually prepare themselves for the "wonders" God would do by separating themselves from things of this world to draw closer to God). This was a *holy* war, requiring spiritual, not military, preparation.
>
> The Ark of the ______________ takes prominence in the narrative, reminding the people of the Lord's presence, His leading them in battle, and paving the way for them to enter the Promised Land. (The Ark is mentioned a full seventeen times in these two chapters, further emphasizing the spiritual significance of the events.)
>
> God's ______________, rather than their military leader, were given the command to take up the Ark and lead the people across.
>
> The Lord promised to __________ Joshua in the sight of the people, so that they would __________ God is with him.
>
> The Jordan River was at flood stage, requiring __divine________ intervention for the entire nation to go safely across (see Joshua 3:15).
>
> Twelve stones, one for each ______________ of Israel, were removed from the Jordan and set up as a ____________.

The purpose of the memorial, as well as the events as a whole, are stated in Joshua 4:24: "so that all the peoples of the earth may know that the hand of the Lord is mighty, that you may fear the Lord your God forever."

PAUSE TO PONDER

Reflect on God's purposes as recorded in Joshua 4:24.
What does it mean to "fear the LORD"? What does this
look like in your own life? What difference does it make that

- all the peoples of the earth may know that the
  hand of the LORD is mighty?

- you may fear the LORD your God forever?

Record your thoughts in the margin or in a journal.

Can you imagine what it must have been like to witness God miraculously pave a way through the roaring Jordan River for the Israelites to cross over into the Promised Land? But little did they know that an even greater challenge lay ahead.

Read Joshua 5:1. How did the kings of the land respond to the events?

How well did their response reflect God's purposes as spoken by Joshua in 4:24?

Try to picture yourself among the Israelites. After generations and generations have waited for the fulfillment of God's promise to Abraham, you are among the first of God's people to take the Promised Land. However, you know the road will not be easy. You are in enemy territory now, and there is no turning back. Everyone is on high alert; a battle awaits. What will the next command be? Sharpen the swords? Practice military drills? After all, the fighting men need to be prepared, strong, and ready for combat. Then the Lord spoke to Joshua. The next command was given. Knives would indeed be sharpened, but when the men heard the reason, jaws dropped in stunned silence.

Read Joshua 5:2–9.

Here is a passage that we might be tempted to gloss over. Generations had been waiting to take the Promised Land; they were so close to victory they could

"You prepare a table before

me in the presence

of my enemies..."

—Psalm 23:5a

taste it. But it seemed God was not in a hurry and considered something else to be far more important: the circumcision of the next generation of Israelites. In one sense, the purpose of the episode is simple and already stated in the text: they had not been circumcised by the prior generation who lived in disobedience and unbelief (Num. 14). But was this the only reason? Let's find out.

> Imagine once again that you are among the Israelites. You just crossed over into enemy territory, and now all the young men are in pain. What might you be
>
> thinking?
>
> feeling?

> Reestablishing circumcision, the mark of the covenant, which God gave to Abraham (Gen. 17:10) and entrusted Moses to keep (Lev. 12:3), served as a sign of renewed commitment to God. Even so, what reasons might God have had for choosing this moment on their journey to require the procedure? (Hint: see Psalm 20:7 in the margin and James 1:3–4 in your Bible.)

"Some trust in chariots and some in horses, but we trust in the name of the Lord our God."

—Psalm 20:7

A Test of Faith

The people had crossed the Jordan. They were surrounded by enemies on every side. We can only imagine some of the people thinking, *Is this really the best time to incapacitate our entire army of fighting men?*

From the outside and our limited perspective (which is quite the understatement), God's ways can seem strange, even foolish, at times. However, God does nothing without a reason. This was partially a test of faith. Their fathers' generation had failed and had even refused to enter the land. Now the next generation had grown up; sadly, even they themselves had failed God (recall Numbers 25:1–3). Nevertheless, God had made a promise to Abraham, and so, in His grace and faithfulness, God led the people into the Promised Land. But the land was still enemy-occupied territory.

One commentator views God's timing as evidence of His grace; by allowing the people to witness God's power in leading them safely across the raging river, they were now "prepared to obey the divine will."[9] Another commentator points out that circumcision was "a necessary precondition for participation in the Passover festival."[10] God was preparing His people, mentally and spiritually, for what lay ahead. Not only is the Passover the next event recorded in the text, but when God first instituted the Passover, the requirement of circumcision was paramount (see Exodus 12:47–48). When we pause to reflect on what was happening when God first gave Abraham the sign of circumcision four hundred years prior, we see the connection even more clearly. In Genesis 17:8–10, God told Abraham,

> And I will give to you and to your offspring after you the land of your sojournings, all the land of Canaan, for an everlasting possession, and I will be their God. . . .
>
> As for you, you shall keep my covenant, you and your offspring after you throughout their generations. This is my covenant, which you shall keep, between me and you and your offspring after you: Every male among you shall be circumcised.

God instituted the covenant sign of circumcision when He promised to give Abraham the Promised Land. Could the people take the land and neglect to keep this covenant sign? Certainly not. But once they obeyed, essentially recommitting themselves to God, then they were ready to take part in the sacred Passover meal.

What is the purpose of the Passover? What does it commemorate? (Hint: glance back at Exodus 12:21–27.)

The Exodus and Passover would become defining events in the identification of God's people as they commemorated God delivering them from slavery while destroying their enemies. But the children of Abraham were not the only ones to find refuge in God. In Exodus 12:38, we read of a "mixed multitude" who feared the Lord and experienced God's mercy by being welcomed into God's covenant community. In the same way, Rahab, a Canaanite prostitute, feared the Lord, experienced God's mercy, and would become a part of God's covenant community.

PAUSE TO PONDER

How have you experienced God's mercy since beginning this study? Be specific.

What impact did it have on your walk with God?

Where are you in need of God's mercy (or grace or protection) right now?

What one truth will you hold on to as you wait for the outcome? Present your petition to God by writing your prayer in the margin or in your journal.

After obeying God's command to reinstate the covenant sign of circumcision, the people had no choice but to wait for the men to heal. We can only imagine how vulnerable the people may have felt. Or perhaps the experience drew the Israelites even closer to God as they reflected on His power to save them, as well as their complete dependence on His protection. But even after the men were healed, before they could move forward in their plans to go to battle against the city of Jericho, another observance was required: Passover.

Read Joshua 5:10-12. Briefly summarize the events.

Read Joshua 3:15. Why was the Jordan overflowing? What time of year (or season) was it?

What significance might the time of year/season have had

in the practical sense? (Hint: see Psalm 37:25.)

in the spiritual sense? (Hint: see Matthew 9:38.)

This was quite a turning point in the history of God's people. Not only had they entered the Promised Land with their enemies trembling in fear, but the miraculous provision of manna (which they had experienced for forty years!) abruptly ceased altogether the very next day after they celebrated Passover. Scripture tells us that the people ate both "unleavened cakes and parched grain" (Josh. 5:11). This means that the Israelites not only ate the grain in the fields, but they also enjoyed food gathered from the prior year's harvest. This food was likely found in storehouses within the small towns outside Jericho whose inhabitants had fled for the safety of the walled city. Here we are given another glimpse of God's faithful provision for His people. Sometimes, He will provide a miracle, and other times, He uses what is readily available. Either way, it all comes from Him.

God Is Our Refuge

Meanwhile, Rahab and her family took refuge in her house, which was tucked inside the city wall. Because the wall around Jericho was the inhabitants' first line of defense, those living in the wall were especially vulnerable during an enemy attack. By this time, many would have sought refuge further within the city.

Try to imagine what it must have been like for Rahab's family as they took refuge in the house of their relative, the prostitute, in a house built within the city wall. Did they second-guess their decision to trust her? Did they personally embrace Rahab's reverence for Israel's God? Could they see the distant Israelite camp from Rahab's window? Did they hear the million-plus Israelite voices singing praises to their God on Passover? If they did, did something in their hearts stir within them?

And what about the sights and sounds of Jericho? Did they hear soldiers shouting? Or babies crying? Or frantic incantations to Canaanite gods? Or maybe all they could hear was silence as fear and dread slithered further into the citizens' minds and hearts. We do not know the details, but we do know that God allowed Himself to be bound by oath to protect Rahab and all who took refuge in her home. In doing so, Rahab's family found refuge in Israel's God. "Blessed is the man who takes refuge in him" (Ps. 34:8)! Amen! Blessed is he indeed!

Throughout the Psalms, numerous promises are made to all of those who take refuge in God. For centuries, God's people have taken comfort in these precious truths. Let's finish today's lesson by looking at just a few.

> "And he gave them the lands of the nations, and they took possession of the fruit of the peoples' toil . . ." —Psalm 105:44

Match each scripture reference in the chart with the promise that best describes it by drawing a line between each pair.

Verse	Promise
Psalm 5:11	Blessed
Psalm 34:8	Mercy
Psalm 34:22	Rest
Psalm 46:1–2	Not condemned
Psalm 57:1	No fear
Psalm 91:1	Sing for joy

...............................YOUR TURN...............................

Ever since the Lord first opened my eyes to His love, the Psalms have been a source of comfort to me. The first psalm I memorized as a new believer was Psalm 91. To this day, it is my favorite go-to passage whenever I am fearful or need a reminder of God's promises.

Which promise(s) from the Psalms in the previous exercise speaks to your heart the most right now? Why?

Share what's on your heart by writing a prayer below.

DAY FOUR
Witnessing Your Old Life Crumble

Because I did not grow up in the church or believing in God, when I became a Christian at the age of thirty, I had a lot to learn. Even the idea that God is real was new to me. I'll never forget the time when I was still a baby believer and went out to dinner with two dear friends. At the end of the meal, the waiter rolled over a display of mouthwatering desserts. My eyes went straight for the chocolate cake. It looked absolutely scrumptious! Even though I wanted that piece of cake, by that time, it was very late, and I was stuffed from dinner, so I reluctantly passed on the chocolate cake.

The next morning at work, I opened the refrigerator, and, to my surprise, I saw an individually wrapped, untouched, mouthwatering piece of gourmet chocolate cake. I was working for a private jet management company at the time, and apparently, a customer had ordered the dessert but had then cancelled their flight. The cake was sitting there in the refrigerator just waiting for someone to enjoy it. I knew immediately that it was for me! My heart soared, and I thought, *God gave me chocolate cake!*

It quickly became a "thing" between my two friends and me. Whenever God would do something special for me, my friends would smile and look at each other, saying, "God gave her chocolate cake." As a baby believer, I was still learning what it meant that God is my loving Father who takes pleasure in delighting His children. For each of us, especially when we are new believers, God often builds our faith by showing Himself in tangible ways as we learn to trust that He is real and is with us. Every so often, He will even use chocolate cake.

Trusting in an Unseen God

Imagine Rahab looking out her window each morning, fingering the scarlet cord dangling from the wooden peg above her window, silently wondering if today would be the day her rescuer was to arrive. The house had become quite crowded. Her nieces and nephews were restless, and her parents were weary as her siblings paced the floor, wondering if they made the right choice, wondering if Israel's God really cared about them. *Will He really come through?* But all any of them could do was wait. Would today be the day of their salvation?

PAUSE TO PONDER

Describe a time when you faced a difficult situation in which you could do nothing but wait—perhaps waiting for test results, or waiting for a jury's verdict, or waiting to learn if you were losing your job or home or a loved one. How did you handle the wait? Were you "greatly shaken" or did you rest on God, "my rock and my salvation" (Ps. 62:2)? Is there anything you would do differently if you had the chance? What would you say to someone facing a similar situation?

The Lord Fights Our Battles

As Rahab and her family waited behind closed doors in Jericho, bracing themselves for the battle to come, Joshua was preparing his men at the Israelite camp. However, before Joshua could lead his men into battle, God had an important message for him.

Before moving forward, let's do a quick review to give us some perspective for what happens next. Three days after Joshua gave the command to cross the Jordan, God miraculously stopped the flow of water, allowing it to rise into a heap far away so the people could cross over on dry ground. Then, after reinstating the covenant sign of circumcision, the people waited three more days for the men to heal. Then, precisely seven days after the command was given to cross, the Israelites celebrated the Passover. This was the fourteenth day of the first month, just as the law required (Exod. 12:1–8).

Nevertheless, a battle was still ahead. Although Joshua had been preparing his 601,730 fighting men both physically and spiritually, God decided it was now Joshua's turn.[11]

> Read Joshua 5:13-14. Compare these verses with Numbers 22:23 and 22:31 and 1 Chronicles 21:16. What similarities do you notice?

The number seven is very significant in the Bible, appearing first in the seven days of creation. The number represents completion.

Who is being described in each and every scene, according to Numbers 22:23 and 22:31 and 1 Chronicles 21:16?

In addition to Joshua 5:13, these are the only other times in the Old Testament where someone appears on the scene with a drawn sword in his hand. This is our first hint at who the visitor in Joshua 5 might be. Let's see what else we can discover.

Read Joshua 5:13-15 (verses 13-14 are review) and then answer the questions.

What was the first thing Joshua asked, and what response was given??

Why do you suppose Joshua's question was not answered? List as many reasons as you can think of.

When Joshua asked the commander of the Lord's army, "Are you for us, or for our adversaries?" (Josh. 5:13) and the commander answered, "No" (Josh. 5:14), his response was nothing less than the message of the gospel! God is not for or against people or nations—He is for righteousness (Matt. 6:33) and against evil, false gods (demons), and everything that entices people to sin. What Joshua did not know at the time was that within Israel's camp was a family of unbelief, and he also failed to consider that within the wicked city was a family of faith. When we consider God's original promise to Abraham that through him "all the families of the earth shall be blessed" (Gen. 12:3), we recognize why the commander did not take sides as Joshua would have expected in light of the impending battle.

Reflect once more on Joshua 5:13-15:

How did Joshua react to the visitor's pronouncement in verse 14? Be specific.

Was Joshua's reverent behavior discouraged?

Consider your answer to the last question. Do you think this is significant? Why or why not?

Let's look at another comparison. Read Revelation 22:8-9. Who was being worshiped?

Contrast how the recipient of worship in Revelation responded with how the recipient of Joshua's worship responded in Joshua 5:14-15.

What conclusions can you draw?

Finally, read Exodus 3:1-5. Below are two sentences extracted from the passage. Fill in the missing titles according to the text.

And the ________________ appeared to him in a flame of fire out of the midst of a bush.

When the ___________ saw that he turned aside to see, ___________ called to him out of the bush, "Moses, Moses!"

Compare Exodus 3:5 with Joshua 5:15. Based on all you have just explored, who might the visitor in Joshua 5 be?

Explain your response.

While some scholars propose that the man (or more accurately, the being who appeared in the likeness of a man) Joshua encountered near Jericho was an angel, others hold that he was a vision of Christ Himself. In Joshua 5:14, we read that Joshua worshiped[12] the divine commander and that Joshua's reverence was not dissuaded. God does not share His glory with anyone. The fact that Joshua's worship was accepted is a strong argument for the visitor being a manifestation of God Himself.

Then there are the striking similarities to Moses's divine encounter in Exodus 3. In both passages, Moses and Joshua hid their faces. Both were commanded to remove their sandals. Both were told that they were standing on holy ground. The ground was not holy because it was somehow different from other lands upon the earth. It was not holy because Moses or Joshua was chosen by God to lead His people. The ground was holy because Moses and Joshua were each standing in the presence of God (specifically, the angel of the Lord). It was here where each man would need courage to embrace his God-given assignment.

Read Joshua 6:1–5. What was Joshua promised, and how would this promise come about?

Some commentators suggest that the words of the Lord, as recorded in Joshua 6:2–5, are a continuation of the words spoken by the commander of the Lord's army. As we explored earlier, a strong case can be made for the commander being the angel of the Lord and, therefore, a manifestation of God Himself. Not only that, but it seems odd for the commander's only instruction to Joshua to be for him to remove his sandals. Either way, Joshua received his marching orders. The Israelites would capture the city not by their might or power or military strategy, but by faith in the Lord's power and His promise of victory.

The Lord Is My Rock and Salvation

For God alone my soul waits in silence; from him comes my salvation.
He alone is my rock and my salvation, my fortress;
I shall not be greatly shaken.

—Psalm 62:1–2

As Joshua and his troops were getting ready to march, Rahab waited with her family for the day of salvation. Finally, she saw them, or perhaps she heard the strange trumpet blasts or soldiers frantically shouting on the top of the city wall,

The Israelites are coming! With her heart pounding in her chest, Rahab ran to her window and looked out. *Wait. Where are their war machines? How will they scale the massive wall? And why are those men blowing trumpets?* None of Rahab's questions were answered. Then, the marching began—*thump, thump, thump.* All the way around the city they marched—close enough to be seen and heard, but just out of reach of any arrows that may have been shot by even the most elite soldiers Jericho's king could muster.

The city held its collective breath, waiting for the first attack. Instead, the Israelites turned and went back the way they came. Maybe the watchmen on the wall squealed in delight, *That's right! Go back where you came from! You and your little horns! You'll never get past our wall!* Or maybe the strange display only caused them to fear all the more, silently dreading what would happen next. Rahab helplessly watched from her window as her rescuers turned and left. Feeling like she'd been punched in the gut, her heart cried out, *No! Don't leave! Surely this is not the end? You promised!* Or maybe the strange display only caused her to pray all the more, eagerly waiting to see what would happen next.

The next day, the Israelites returned. Trumpets blew and soldiers marched, same as the day before. We can imagine Rahab's family, perhaps demanding of Rahab, *What are they doing out there? I thought you said they would come for us. Why all this marching?* But Rahab had no answers. All she could do was trust in the One who promised to save her.

Six days went by with the same routine, as over six hundred thousand men marched around the city. Even Rahab's nieces and nephews tired of the spectacle. It seemed it would never end, but then, on the seventh day, the Israelites arrived far earlier than they had in prior days. Something was about to change.

......................................YOUR TURN......................................

God never promised that being His follower would be easy. Jesus told His disciples, "In the world you will have tribulation. But take heart; I have overcome the world" (John 16:33).

Where in your life right now are you facing a battle?

In what ways are you taking refuge in God?

In what ways do you need to take refuge in God, and what may be standing in the way?

If you are blessed to not be facing a difficulty or struggle at this time, what can you do to prepare for the battles that will inevitably come your way?

DAY FIVE
He Knows My Name

One of the things my friends know about me is that I love spending time at the beach. The rhythm of the waves and warm gentle breezes do wonders for clearing my thoughts and calming my soul. Because I live near the ocean, one day each week (as long as the weather is nice), I head to the beach for a "Sabbath date with Jesus."

I follow a regular routine: after arriving at the beach and setting up my blanket, umbrella, and chair, I silence my phone and zip it in a pocket on the beach chair. My aim is to unplug; the phone is there only for emergencies. I spend the day reading, taking leisurely walks along the shore, journaling, or simply watching the waves, seabirds, and the occasional pod of dolphins swimming by. I can easily spend up to eight hours on the beach, as I always pack a lunch and plenty of snacks in my backpack to carry me through until the last glimpses of the sunset signal it's time to head home.

After one long day at the beach, I was folding up the beach chair when it completely fell apart. It seems that after several years of sun and sand, it was time to be replaced. On the way to my car, I stopped at a large dumpster near the welcome center and heaved the chair into the dumpster. The leisurely day always ends with a forty-minute drive home as I sing along to the songs playing on our local Christian radio station.

"He drew me up from the pit of destruction, out of the miry bog, and set my feet upon a rock . . . He put a new song in my mouth, a song of praise to our God." —Psalm 40:2-3

God always knows where you are, and because you belong to Him, He will come for you—no matter where you are or what you've done.

It wasn't until I arrived home and began unpacking my backpack that I realized my phone was nowhere to be found. I went out to the car and reached my hand under each seat, only to find some gas receipts, a key chain, and an old french fry (I can only guess how long it had been there, but it looked the same as if I had bought it that morning). Back to my search. I scoured every corner of the car, but still no phone. I went back inside my home and logged on to my computer, where I shared my predicament on social media. A friend messaged me, reminding me that if I hadn't powered down my phone, I might be able to find it using the "Find My" app. I forgot about the app, as I had never needed it before. I opened the app, and sure enough, my phone was still at the beach. In fact, it was right by the welcome center. Only then did I realize that I had left the phone in the beach chair pocket, the chair I had tossed into a dumpster. However, it was now evening. I knew there was nothing I could do but wait until the next day.

The following morning, I opened the app again and watched in horror as my iPhone tracker showed my phone slowly moving away from its last location. Not having a cell phone or a landline, I quickly messaged the welcome center on social media and explained the situation. After several agonizing minutes, I get a message back: the dumpster had just been picked up, but they were sending someone to try and stop the truck, find the chair, and retrieve my phone. That's some impressive customer service!

In the end, my phone was saved, and I gave the hero a cash reward. As I was driving home from the beach a second time, God used the events to show me an analogy. Isn't it curious how God can use almost any situation to teach us something? I pictured the phone—as valuable as it was— as lost, trapped, and discarded in a dumpster. But as its owner, I knew exactly where it was. It didn't matter to me that it was in a dumpster; it was still of great worth in my sight.

PAUSE TO PONDER

Have you ever experienced a time when you felt lost or trapped, perhaps as though you had been thrown in a dumpster? Looking back, did God abandon you there? How can you take comfort in knowing that God "will never leave you nor forsake you" (Heb. 13:5)? He always knows where you are, and because you belong to Him, He will come for you—no matter where you are or what you've done.

I Call You by Name

Read 2 Peter 3:9 and 2 Timothy 2:19. How do these verses shed light on the events we have been studying over the past few weeks?

"The Lord knows those who are his" (2 Tim. 2:19). Of all the people we have encountered in the events so far, it is significant to note that Rahab is the only citizen of Jericho named in the Bible *and* the only person in the city who had a reverential "fear of the LORD." Isaiah 43:1 refers to those redeemed by the Lord: "I have called you by name, you are mine." Giving a name to someone (such as a parent naming a child or a wife taking the family name of her husband) conveys relationship. With God, it's a sign of His covenant relationship to His people. God calls us by name.

Though Rahab had been living as a prostitute in a wicked city, her faith in God meant that Rahab and her family now belonged to Him. While God knew where Rahab and her family were hidden, their deliverance was yet to come. Meanwhile, Joshua was about to receive his battle plans—and they sounded nothing like anything he could have imagined.

Read Joshua 6:1–21 (verses 1–5 are review). As you read, record how many times these words appear in the chapter:

Seven/seventh_____________

Trumpet(s)_______________

While the word "seven" occurs frequently in the Bible (nearly four hundred times!), there is only one other place in the Bible where we encounter a high frequency of "seven(s)" and "trumpet(s)" occurring together: the book of Revelation. That book includes fifty-five mentions of seven(s) and fourteen mentions of trumpet(s), with all but two trumpet references being associated with God's righteous wrath and judgment.[14] We will come back to Revelation in Week Six, but since we are on the subject, here's a fun question to ponder:

Based on what you may have read or heard about the book of Revelation, what concepts, characters, or imagery from Revelation come to mind that also appear in the story of Rahab from the chapters we have been studying in Joshua? List as many as you can think of.

The ram's horn and trumpet (same instrument) produced only a few notes and was used mainly as a signal. Here it signaled God's presence and announced Jericho's impending doom.[13]

One of the things I love about the Bible is how all of it is interconnected. There is simply no passage in all of Scripture that, with careful examination and proper exegesis, does not connect to other passages, with all of Scripture ultimately pointing us to Christ. The story of Rahab in the book of Joshua is no exception, and its parallels in the book of Revelation are no coincidence. But before we explore those further in Week Six, we still have a few more passages to cover in Joshua. I assure you that we do not want to miss them!

The Lord's Portion

For six days, the priests carried the Ark of the Covenant around Jericho while sounding seven trumpets. For some, these trumpets served as an announcement of impending judgment.[15] For others—namely, Rahab and her family hidden within the city wall—they were the sound of imminent salvation! Finally, on the seventh day, Joshua commanded the people: "Shout, for the LORD has given you the city" (Josh. 6:16). But with the victory came a warning.

Reread Joshua 6:17–19. What warning did Joshua give to the Israelites regarding the "devoted things," according to verse 18?

Further, what were Joshua's instructions regarding

the city and all that was within it (apart from Rahab and the precious metals)?

Rahab?

items of silver, gold, bronze, and iron?

Unlike future conquests of other Canaanite cities, Joshua and the people were strictly warned to take no plunder from Jericho for themselves. A number of scholars propose that the reason is that the entire city of Jericho was symbolically a kind of firstfruits to the Lord.[16] One commentator explains, "God's command that they devote the city of Jericho to Him was similar to His command to give Him the first fruits of the harvest. Whenever Israel disobeyed this command, the effects were disastrous."[17]

Being that the city was the first in the conquest for the Promised Land, its destruction would also serve as a testimony to God's power and as an example to other nations of His sovereignty. Further, all items of valuable metals were to be placed in the treasury of the Lord. There were at least three reasons why God prohibited the Israelites from taking anything valuable for themselves. First, the treasury was used in part to provide for the needs of God's people, so that there would be no poor or needy persons among them. Second, these items were "holy to the LORD" (Josh. 6:19) and belonged to Him alone. Third, this was a holy war. God was teaching His people that the battle was won not by man's power or wisdom, but by God's. At the proper time, the men would shout a war cry, but it was God who turned the wall to dust.[18]

God alone owned the land—all the land. God also promised to give a portion of the land to Abraham and his descendants. By requiring the Israelites to, in a sense, give back to the Lord the first portion of the land in the conquest, the people were reminded that even future cities in which they would be permitted to plunder all belonged to Him, and He could give it to whomever He pleased.

Read Joshua 6:22–25.

Based on this passage, which is presented from Joshua's viewpoint at the time, were Joshua's instructions obeyed concerning each of the following? (Circle yes or no).

The city and all that was within it (apart from Rahab and the precious metals)

Yes   No

Rahab

Yes   No

Items of silver, gold, bronze, and iron

Yes   No

Imagine being a member of Israel's army heading into battle with the command to devote everything in the city to destruction, which meant "both men and women, young and old, oxen, sheep, and donkeys" (Josh. 6:21). What challenges might you have faced?

What would you need to be able to move forward in this conquest?

If God asked you today to do something that felt extremely difficult or even distressing, what would help you move forward in obedience?

To our modern sensibilities, God's decree to destroy all the people, including children, may be difficult for us to understand, even though it was decreed by God to Abraham hundreds of years beforehand (Gen. 15:16; see also Deuteronomy 7:1–5 and 20:16–18 and Leviticus 18:24–25 and 20:23–24). However, God's command to "show no mercy" (Deut. 7:2) did not mean that the Israelites were to feel vindictive toward the Canaanites; rather, they were supposed to feel motivated toward themselves.[19] By commanding His people to clear the Promised Land of wickedness, the Israelites were instrumental in establishing a place for God's name—rather than false "gods" (or demons)—on the earth. At the same time, the task could not have been easy for everyone. It was in times like these when a strong faith and firm recognition of who God is (His holiness, goodness, justice, mercy—as was shown to Rahab) are what would carry them through any God-given assignment.

As we wrestle with God's ways, we need to be careful not to minimize God's mercy and grace toward Rahab and her family. Jericho was a fortified city. Only the spies who had visited Rahab could possibly have had any hope (apart from divine guidance) of finding her home in the midst of the demolished walls, deafening screams, clouds of dust, and ensuing chaos—not to mention keeping themselves safe from enemy attack as the city's soldiers and leaders fought in vain to save themselves (see Joshua 24:11).

In God's providence, Joshua sent the spies into the city to rescue Rahab. When we take the time to examine the structure of the text, we discover that God's salvation of Rahab and her family, rather than the destruction of those remaining

in the city, was the writer's primary focus. As such, this needs to be our focus as well. We will take a closer look at this as we begin next week's lesson.

......................................YOUR TURN......................................

Next to each verse below, write your name in the space provided. Now read each verse, beginning with your name, out loud.

________, the Lord . . . is patient toward you, not wishing that any should perish, but that all should reach repentance. —2 Peter 3:9

________, the Lord knows those who are his. —2 Timothy 2:19

________, I have called you by name, you are mine. —Isaiah 43:1

Which of these truths do you need to be reminded of today?

Spend a few moments in prayer with your heavenly Father; speak back to God each verse that you need to remember today.

Write your prayer below.

Lesson Summary

What scripture, statement, or thought was most significant to you this week? Write it down, and then reword it into a prayer of response to God.

Notes

[1]"Signal," in *Lexham Analytical Lexicon of the Hebrew Bible* (Bellingham, WA: Lexham Press, 2017).

[2]These "first" and "second" references to a scarlet cord or thread relate to biblical accounts where they have a prominent place in a narrative involving specific people or key events. For our purposes, Old Testament references to scarlet yarn or thread used in the fabrics of the tabernacle or priestly garments are not included here.

[3]Earl D. Radmacher, Ronald Barclay Allen, and H. Wayne House, eds., *Nelson's NKJV Study Bible*, Josh. 3:2 (Nashville: Thomas Nelson, 1997).

[4]*ESV Study Bible* (Wheaton, IL: Crossway, 2008), 397.

[5]Curiously, an interruption to the narrative is exactly how Tamar's story in Genesis 38 is positioned in the Bible. Like the story of Rahab interrupting the taking of the Promised Land, Tamar's story interrupts the story of Joseph, which is left hanging in Genesis 37 and picks up right where it left off in Genesis 39.

[6]Jerome F. D. Creach, "Joshua," in *Interpretation: A Bible Commentary for Teaching and Preaching* (Louisville, KY: Westminster John Knox Press, 2003), 43 [quoted: Hoffman, "The Deuteronomistic Concept of Herem," 197].

[7]N. Scott Amos and Timothy George, eds., *Joshua, Judges, Ruth*, Reformation Commentary on Scripture: Old Testament, vol. 4 (Downers Grove, IL: InterVarsity Press Academic, 2020), 45.

[8]Kenneth O. Gangel, *Joshua*, Holman Old Testament Commentary, ed. Max Anders (Nashville: B&H, 2002), 34.

[9]Robert Jamieson, A. R. Fausset, and David Brown, *Commentary Critical and Explanatory on the Whole Bible*, vol. 1 (Oak Harbor, WA: Logos Research Systems, 1997), 146.

[10]Marten H. Woudstra, *The Book of Joshua*, The New International Commentary on the Old Testament (Grand Rapids: Eerdmans, 1981), 102.

[11]See Numbers 26:1–2, 51.

[12]Some translations say "bowed down," but since we are already told Joshua "fell on his face to the earth," "worshiped" is a better representation of what is happening here.

[13]Radmacher, Allen, House, *Nelson's NKJV Study Bible*, Josh. 6:5.

[14]The two exceptions are Revelation 1:10 and 4:1, where John describes the divine voice he hears as sounding "like a trumpet."

[15]Warren Austin Gage, *Gospel Typology in Joshua and Revelation* (Fort Lauderdale: St. Andrews House, 2013).

[16]Several examples include: Jamieson, Fausset, and Brown, *Commentary Critical and Explanatory on the Whole Bible*, vol. 1, 147; John Calvin and Henry Beveridge, *Commentary on the Book of Joshua* (Bellingham, WA: Logos Bible Software, 2010), 95; and *ESV Study Bible*, 401.

[17]Radmacher, Allen, and House, *Nelson's NKJV Study Bible*, Josh. 6:17–18.

[18]Very likely, the wall fell in a manner that provided numerous openings for the Israelite soldiers to walk straight into the city but left enough of the wall standing to prevent the people of Jericho from escaping. This also explains why Rahab's house remained intact enough to keep her and her family safe until they were rescued. The importance of the event is not that every inch of the wall crumbled, but that it crumbled by an act of God.

[19]John H. Walton and J. Harvey Walton, *The Lost World of the Israelite Conquest: Covenant, Retribution, and the Fate of the Canaanites* (Downers Grove, IL: InterVarsity Press Academic, 2017), 242.

PART III

THE PRICE

TESTIFYING TO THE HOPE OF SALVATION

RAHAB AND HER FAMILY WERE RESCUED AND PLACED outside the camp. After a period of separation, they entered the community of God's people. Imagine Rahab's shock as she witnessed the execution of one of God's own for daring to take some of the "devoted things" (Josh. 6:18). Yet where a son of Israel was cut off, the prostitute Rahab was grafted in.

Sadly, it would not take long before many Israelites turned to other gods. In a remarkable contrast, when it comes to the New Testament's "honor roll of faith," it is Rahab's name that we find there.

DAY ONE
Living between Two Worlds

I did not grow up going to church or believing in God. I was thirty years old when I first heard the gospel. I had a lot of questions, but God was patient with me. Six months later, God mercifully opened my eyes to see the truth. In His love, He sent His Son to save me from my sins. Had someone told me at that time that God would one day call me to seminary and to serve Him as a Bible teacher, I would have laughed out loud. With my shameful past, I could never have imagined that God would choose someone like me. Sound familiar?

As I shared in Week Two, I was a young teen when I started abusing drugs and alcohol. By the time I was seventeen years old, I began going to nightclubs. Because I loved to dance, every night at the club was one big party. Dancing. Drinking. Flirting. If you had asked me then if I was having fun, I confess that I would have answered with a resounding "Yes!" Some nights I even brought my camera. I took pictures almost everywhere I went, including on family vacations and at parties with friends. If I was having fun, I wanted pictures to hold on to the memories. It seemed only natural to have pictures of my friends and me partying at the clubs. But soon the nightclub scene opened the door to more poor choices. Drinking led to harder drugs. Flirting led to sleeping with men I hardly knew.

Years later, after God called me to follow Him, I was looking for something in my closet and came across those old photo albums. Seeing the pictures of me dancing in bars with a haughty smile on my face, I was repulsed. I began to tear up the photographs. I did this not out of anger, but shame.

Tearing up the photos was a tangible reminder that my old life is past; I am no longer who I once was. Even so, there are things that still remind me of my past. To this day, I am very selective about the kind of music I listen to. Music and lyrics have a powerful effect on a person's thoughts and emotions (God designed us that way). For me, the wrong kind of music and suggestive lyrics immediately bring to mind nightclub scenes and memories of my shameful past. That's what sin does: first it entices us, then it degrades us, then it condemns us. As I looked at the photographs, I knew I could not erase my past, but I decided I did not need to hold on to it, either.

PAUSE TO PONDER

Since becoming a Christian, what areas from your past have you let go of? Was your victory over this area immediate, or did it take time? What impact did your journey of letting go have on your relationship with God? Is there a negative influence from your past that you are you still struggling with? What one step can you take to gain victory in this area?

> That's what sin does: first it entices us, then it degrades us, then it condemns us. Praise God for our victory over sin through Christ!

Being Made New

If you belong to Christ, the Bible promises that you have been made new (2 Cor. 5:17). Just as I had to let go of my past and Rahab had to let go of hers, your past no longer defines who you are. And the best part? God is with you!

Read 2 Corinthians 5:17 in the margin. What is necessary before someone can become a "new creation," according to this verse?

What does becoming a "new creation" look like? (Hint: see Romans 8:29 and Colossians 3:9–10.)

Consider what you were like before you became a Christian and who you are today. (If you became a Christian at a very early age, reflect on how God has changed you over the past ten years or so.) For each area below that applies to you, describe one specific way your new life as a Christian has made a difference:

your personal life

your marriage or family

your church

your social circle

your work or school or ministry

other______________

Here is an encouraging insight from the original Greek text. The verb "to become" in the phrase "all things have become new" in 2 Corinthians 5:17 is in a Greek verb form called perfect active indicative. This means that the author is making a statement of fact[1] concerning an action that was completed at a point of time in the past and also continues to unfold in the present.

In other words, as a child of God, there was a point in your life when you became a "new creation." At the same time, as long as you and I live in our sinful bodies in a wicked, broken world, we will still wrestle to live out this truth of being made new each day until we enter our eternal home. But consider this: in the spiritual realm, it is already accomplished! When God, who exists outside of time, looks at you, He sees you completely made new—sinless, spotless, and pure in His eyes. Right here. Right now. Right where you are. You are breathtakingly beautiful in His sight.

PAUSE TO PONDER

Reflecting on your life since becoming a new creation:

What old things (beliefs, desires, habits) have passed away?

What new things have risen in their place?

Take a few moments to give God praise for refusing to leave you just the way you are, for His commitment, and for empowerment through His Holy Spirit living within you, to make you a new creation.

Outside the Camp

At the end of Week Four, I mentioned that the structure of the text in Joshua 6 helps us to see that the focus of the passage is not on the destruction of the masses, but on God's grace in saving Rahab and her family. Let's look at the passage a little more closely.

Joshua 6:17–25 is written, in part, below. Underline each mention of the city and what will happen (or has happened) to it. Next, place a circle around each mention of Rahab and what will happen (or has happened) to her and her family. I completed the first underline one for you.

And <u>the city and all that is within it shall be devoted to the Lord for destruction</u>. Only Rahab the prostitute and all who are with her in her house shall live, because she hid the messengers whom we sent. . . . Then they devoted all in the city to destruction, both men and women, young and old, oxen, sheep, and donkeys, with the edge of the sword.

But to the two men who had spied out the land, Joshua said, "Go into the prostitute's house and bring out from there the woman and all who belong to her, as you swore to her." So the young men who had been spies went in and brought out Rahab and her father and mother and brothers and all who belonged to her. . . .

And they burned the city with fire, and everything in it. . . . But Rahab the prostitute and her father's household and all who belonged to her, Joshua saved alive.

How many times are the people of the city mentioned compared with the number of times Rahab and her family are mentioned?

The people of the city are mentioned _________ time(s).

Rahab and her family are mentioned _________ time(s).

Did you notice a pattern in the text? Explain. (Hint: How are each of the underlined and circled segments of the text positioned in relation to one another?)

What conclusions can you draw based on what you discovered in the previous questions?

Three times, we read of the city's destruction (or impending destruction). Each of these three pronouncements are followed by an assurance that Rahab and her family were to be spared. Each and every time. This helps us recognize that the emphasis of the passage is not on those who perish, but on those who live!

One commentary author writes, "Rahab's salvation is evidence that Joshua's authors themselves were concerned about the implications of the [command to destroy everything and everyone in the city] and so presented the ban as a backdrop for what was most important, namely, a presentation of God's salvation and rescue [of Rahab] from destruction."[2]

Reread Joshua 6:22–24. What happened to Rahab and her family after they were rescued from the city? Be specific.

"For 'everyone who calls on the name of the Lord will be saved.'" —Romans 10:13

List one or two reasons why they would not have immediately been assimilated into the Israelite community. (Hint: see Deuteronomy 7:1–5 and Leviticus 18:24–25.)

Try to imagine yourself in Rahab's sandals. You are not yet permitted to enter the Israelite camp in front of you, but behind you, you can hear the screams and see the smoke rising to the heavens as your city, your home, and all that was once familiar burn to the ground. What might you be

thinking?

feeling?

To say that Rahab and her family were grateful to be saved from death would be quite an understatement. But surely they would be wondering what would happen to them next. We are not told how long the family was kept outside the camp, but there are several reasons why this was necessary. One of these would be to protect the community from any dangerous influences that Rahab and her family might bring, even if unintentionally. Let's explore several other reasons.

Read the following verses in your Bible. What common message is being conveyed?

Isaiah 52:11   2 Corinthians 6:17–18   Revelation 18:4

Next, read Leviticus 13:45–46 and Numbers 5:2–3. What was one way the Israelites were instructed to deal with community members who were "unclean"?

How do the verses in the previous two questions shed light on Rahab's situation?

God repeatedly called His people to come out from wicked cities or separate themselves from the wicked or unclean (Isa. 52:11; Jer. 51:6; 2 Cor. 6:17; Rev. 18:4). In biblical times, anyone considered "unclean" must be placed outside the camp. Even though being "unclean" typically referred to physical ailments, Psalm 51 reminds us that it is our sin that makes us unclean: "Have mercy on me, O God, according to your steadfast love; according to your abundant mercy blot out my transgressions. Wash me thoroughly from my iniquity, and cleanse me from my sin" (Ps. 51:1–2)!

If Rahab and her family had been allowed to walk right into the Israelite camp, they might never have recognized the need to intentionally reject their former way of life (and, spiritually speaking, to be cleansed). The effects of decades of living in a wicked, idolatrous city would not disappear in a day. By being placed outside the camp, Rahab and her family would have had no choice but to face the shame of their past. But even this was an act of God's grace, as Rahab and her family were given time to repent of their past before they were prepared to become a part of God's covenant nation.

YOUR TURN

Have you ever heard someone say (or perhaps you've said it yourself), "God loves you just the way you are"?

What motivation might compel someone to say this to another person? (Perhaps you have even said this to yourself.)

Try to ponder the statement from God's point of view. Does it still hold up?

Explain.

> "Therefore go out from their midst, and be separate from them, says the Lord, and touch no unclean thing; then I will welcome you, and I will be a father to you ..."
> —2 Corinthians 6:17–18

God certainly does love us. The Bible not only says so, but from a post-cross vantage point, you and I are witnesses of the extent of His great love for us. But to say He loves us "just the way we are" is to essentially say Christ died for nothing. God loves us, but He loves us in spite of the way we are. He loves us so much that He refuses to abandon us to stay as we are. For Rahab and her family, they may have been rescued from death, but their decision to follow and obey the Holy One of Israel for the rest of their lives was no small matter. But oh, it was worth it!

Day Two
Witnessing the Price of Sin

Yesterday, we finished our lesson by wrapping up Joshua 6, where we read that "Rahab the prostitute and her father's household . . . Joshua saved alive" (Josh. 6:25). What a glorious testament to God's faithfulness! But the writer was not finished; he completed his thought by adding, "And she has lived in Israel to this day . . ." (Josh. 6:25).

The last part of the verse reminds us of Rahab's future genealogy as being in the lineage of Christ. However, at the time the book of Joshua was written, these words most likely simply reflected the fact that Rahab was still living among the Israelites at the time. The statement was included as a way of authenticating the story by reminding the people that Rahab was still alive and living with them at the time the book of Joshua was written. It was as if to say, *If you do not believe me, you can go and speak with Rahab herself.* Oh, don't you wish we could do just that? We'll need to wait for heaven for that day, and we'll probably have to wait in line!

While Joshua 6:25 is the last time Rahab's name appears in the Old Testament, as we will discover in the days ahead, her story is far from over.

Consider all we have read in Joshua 6 up to this point. Is the scarlet cord ever mentioned again?

Do you find this curious? Disappointing? Share your thoughts.

Before writing this study, the scarlet cord had always been at the forefront of Rahab's story in my mind. And I know I am not the only one. Although the scarlet

Interesting Fact: Most, if not all, of the book of Joshua was written during Rahab's lifetime; it is one of the earliest written segments of the entire Old Testament.

cord did not save Rahab, it identified her (and her home) as being set apart for God's special protection. Very often, in discussing the story of Rahab, the scarlet cord is thought to point to the blood of Christ. That may certainly be the case. However, in addition to that symbolism, there is something else in the text we do not want to overlook: the oath of protection the spies made to Rahab also had much to do with the door of her house (Josh. 2:17–21).

The men warned her, "Then if anyone goes out of the doors of your house into the street, his blood shall be on his own head, and we shall be guiltless. But if a hand is laid on anyone who is with you in the house, his blood shall be on our head" (Josh. 2:19). This brings to mind the door of Noah's ark, which protected the family from flood (Gen 6:16, 7:16), the door of Lot's house, which protected the family from the city's wicked men (Gen 19:10), and the door of the Passover, which, marked with blood, protected those families from the angel of death (Exod. 12:7, 12:13).[3] In every case, God appointed a door of safety on the day of judgment. This is evidence of God's saving grace. All who were outside the door perished.[4] This is why Jesus could declare in John's Gospel, "I am the door. If anyone enters by me, he will be saved . . ." (John 10:9).

However, today we will discover that, although neither the scarlet cord nor Rahab's name are specifically mentioned again in the story, both still speak. In fact, they speak volumes. To see the scarlet cord's place in the continuation of Rahab's story, we need to take a look at the events in Joshua 7.

Welcome to the Family

After a transition period, Rahab and her family were accepted into God's covenant nation. By the time the book of Joshua was written, Rahab had become an established member of the community. Her faith in God and in His promise saved her and her entire family from destruction. Sadly, in the very next chapter following the account of Rahab's rescue, we discover that not everyone took God at His word.

Printed below is the first verse of Joshua 7, copied from the English Standard Version. Fill in the missing words or phrases based on the passage.

But the people of Israel __________ in regard to the devoted things, for Achan the son of Carmi . . . of the tribe of __________, took some of the devoted things. And the anger of the Lord __________ against the people of Israel.

"Come, my people, enter your chambers, and shut your doors behind you; hide yourselves for a little while until the fury has passed by." —Isaiah 26:20

Since the crime was committed by a single individual, why do you think the Lord was angry with the whole community? List as many reasons as you can think of.

Though the sin was committed by one man, soon the whole community would suffer. Meanwhile, Joshua, being unaware of the situation, sent his men to capture the next territory in Canaan, a small city named Ai.

Read Joshua 7:2–5. Whose counsel did Joshua listen to? Circle one.

God   men

Reflect on your answer to the last question. Do you think Joshua's decision had any impact on the outcome of his military attack on Ai? Place an X on the line to indicate your response.

No impact   Great impact

Explain your response.

PAUSE TO PONDER

When making important decisions, all of us have made the mistake of moving forward in our own strength and wisdom at one time or another. How might your life be different if you brought every important decision to the Lord before moving forward? Be specific.

When Joshua sent his men, numbering around three thousand, to attack Ai, instead of the expected victory, the Israelites returned humiliated. Some even lost their lives. When the report of their utter defeat reached the camp, we read that the "hearts of the people melted [in fear]" (Josh. 7:5)—just as the hearts of the people of Jericho had melted in fear of the Israelites just one battle earlier. Stunned, Joshua cried out to the Lord.

Read Joshua 7:6–7. Who did Joshua blame for Israel's defeat at Ai?

Why do you think Joshua responded this way?

Read Joshua 7:10–11. Who did God blame for Israel's defeat at Ai?

What reasons did God give? Be specific.

Read Joshua 7:12. List the consequences Joshua and the people would suffer as a result of their sin. Be specific.

How were obedience and victory over the enemy connected, according to the passages you just read?

Contrast Joshua 6:27 with Joshua 7:12. What remedy did the Lord prescribe to restore His favor and presence to Joshua and the people?

Read Joshua 7:13–15, and then answer the questions.

How did the Lord describe the man's crimes, according to verse 15? Fill in the blank to complete the phrase: *he has transgressed the* __________ *of the* Lord.

The first thing the Lord told Joshua was to consecrate (or "sanctify" in some translations) the people. Look up the word *consecrate* in a Bible dictionary or regular dictionary. Write the meaning below.

What did the Lord's command to consecrate the people imply about the community's spiritual condition?

Consider the Lord's pronouncement in verse 15. Do you find it to be harsh? Why or why not?

The city of Jericho and everything in it was "devoted . . . for destruction" (Josh. 6:17). Valuable items such as precious metals would be placed in the treasury of the Lord. These items were "holy to the LORD" (Josh. 6:19), meaning that they were holy and should not be handled carelessly.[5]

While the man and his family suffered a terrible fate, this sort of tragedy is never again recorded in the book of Joshua. However, the focus of the story is not on the loss of this family. Here's another Bible study tip: when reading about difficult events, such as the annihilation of the Canaanites or the execution of Achan and his family, if the text does not depict an event as an atrocity, then we cannot claim that it was an atrocity.[6] Were the events tragic? Yes. Unjust? No.

If this were a civil case, only the individual would be held liable (Deut. 24:16). The fact that God began His response to Joshua with a demand that all the people consecrate themselves reveals that this was both a religious offense and a corporate one—an offense that, if not purged, would pollute the entire community. According to the Lord's last words to Joshua in Joshua 7:15, the man had done "an outrageous thing" in Israel. The Hebrew word translated "outrageous thing" is *nebalah*. This word only appears a handful of times in the Old Testament and almost without exception relates to events involving rape, sodomy, or adultery, including spiritual adultery (see Genesis 34:7; Deuteronomy 22:21; 2 Samuel 13:12; Jeremiah 29:23). As a result of taking the "devoted things," which belonged to the Lord alone, the man effectively sealed himself and his family with the same fate God pronounced on the "devoted things": destruction.

.................................YOUR TURN.................................

Are there any "devoted things" (or areas of unbelief/disobedience) in your life that might be

hindering you from experiencing victory?

making you vulnerable to the enemy's attack?

How might holding on to these "devoted things" be injuring those around you?

Bible study tip: if a proper reading of the text and imagery does not depict an event as an atrocity, divine judgment, punishment for sin, or even divine mercy, then we cannot claim that these are occurring, either.

Ask the Lord to help you identify, confess, and surrender these "devoted things." Write a prayer as God leads you.

DAY THREE
Hearing the Words of Life

Yesterday, we read of the Israelites' surprising and crushing defeat in their effort to capture the city of Ai. When Joshua directed his frustration at God, he discovered that the problem was within his own camp. Someone had defied God's command by daring to take some of the "devoted things" for himself.

A Twist of Fate

God did not simply call out (or inform Joshua of) the guilty party by name. He could have. Instead, God required Joshua to identify the offender by a series of taking lots. First, he was to identify the tribe (the people of Israel were identified as belonging to one of twelve tribes, which were descended from the twelve sons of Jacob). Next, the clan (or family or household) to which the guilty party belonged would be identified (clans were the groups descended from each son born to each of the twelve sons of Jacob). On the surface, the purpose of the exercise may simply appear to be a process of elimination—and it was. But by identifying the tribe and the clan, Scripture is revealing to us something else—something very important.

Read Joshua 7:16–26. Briefly summarize the events.

To which tribe did the man belong, according to verse 16?

To which clan (family) did the man belong, according to verse 17?

Do you recognize the name of this clan? Complete Genesis 38:30 on the following page.

Interesting Fact: In Hebrew, *Ai* means ruins.[7]

Shinar was a region of Mesopotamia that, at various times, included Babel, and later, the city of Babylon, areas associated with rebellion and idolatry (see Genesis 10:10, 11:1–9; Daniel 1:1–2).

Afterward his brother came out with ______________________

____

____.

Glance back at Joshua 6:17 and 6:25. What reason is given for Rahab and her family being saved? Check one.

- ☐ Rahab's faith
- ☐ God's faithfulness
- ☐ Rahab hiding the messengers

Even though the Bible only mentions one of the reasons listed in the previous question, how are all three interconnected?

Although Rahab was recognized for her actions, it was God's reputation at stake. At the end of the day, Rahab was saved because God kept His promise, which was given to her by oath through His two messengers. God always keeps His promises. At the same time, it was Rahab's faith (revealed in her profound profession in chapter 2) that gave her the courage to hide the messengers in the first place—the very thing she is specifically remembered for. Being convinced that Yahweh was the true "God in the heavens above and on the earth beneath," Rahab and her family (because of Rahab's witness) "put their trust in the sign of God's promise, taking refuge in a scarlet cord"[8] rather than in armies and walls and weapons. Yet even here, we are forced to acknowledge that, apart from God's faithfulness, no one will be saved.

Complete the table by comparing and contrasting the faith and fate of Achan and Rahab. I filled in one for you.

	Faith/Fear of the Lord (reverent or irreverent)	Fate/Outcome of the Person and Their Family (life or death)
Rahab	*reverent*	
Achan		

How are faith (fear of the Lord) and fate (outcome, consequences) connected in the story of

Rahab?

Achan?

What general principles can you apply to your own life?

The stories of Rahab and Achan are not independent of one another; in fact, Scripture presents a striking connection. However, for us to see it clearly, we need to briefly take a look at two additional passages.

Read Matthew 1:1–5. Who did Rahab marry?

Which son of Judah and Tamar was Rahab's husband descended from? Circle one.

Perez   Zerah

Which son of Judah and Tamar had the scarlet thread tied on his wrist? Circle one. (Hint: glance back at Genesis 38:30.)

Perez   Zerah

Let's pause here for a moment and consider once again Achan's crime and the manner in which the guilty party was discovered. First, his tribe was taken (chosen by lot), then his clan, then his household, then each man. God gave Achan at least four opportunities to come forward and confess his crime. Perhaps God would have been merciful. Instead, Achan kept silent until his secret was exposed and he could hide no longer. Only then did he confess, but there was nothing to indicate a true change of heart.

In the end, the entire family line of Achan, a descendant of Zerah, the supposed firstborn of Judah and Tamar, was destroyed and forever cut off from God's covenant family. But how could that be? Zerah was the one wearing the scarlet cord—the sign of redemption. Where was the redemption? To answer this question, we need only look to the scarlet cord silently hanging in Rahab's window—a window from which a Canaanite prostitute delivered two men of Israel in exchange for saving her from the death sentence hanging over her. The allusions to the story of Tamar cannot be ignored: Tamar, a Canaanite disguised as a prostitute,

Of all the people God could have chosen to foreshadow the bride He would select for His Son, God chose a redeemed Canaanite prostitute.

Interesting Fact: Joshua 8:28 records that the city of Ai was a heap of ruins "to this day"—another reminder to the original readers that these events were verifiable at the time Joshua was written (see also Joshua 13:13, 23:9).

sentenced to death, who instead delivered two sons of Israel from her womb, and in the end was grafted into God's covenant family. "While the midwife of Tamar tied the scarlet cord of election upon Zerah, God's marvelous providence overrode the convention of the midwife, tying the scarlet cord of election upon *Rahab*!"[9]

Isn't God's Word amazing?! Rahab, who was a kind of firstfruits of the Promised Land, was given as her bridegroom a descendant of Tamar's son Perez. In one sense, she was grafted into the exact place where Achan was cut off. Even more astonishing is that God placed both Tamar and Rahab into the very royal line of David and Christ Himself![10] Of all the people God could have chosen to foreshadow the bride He would select for His Son, God chose a redeemed Canaanite prostitute. Wow.

I can hardly wait until we get to Week Six, where we will see how all of the key concepts we have been studying tie into the bigger picture. Remember what I shared in Week Two: Rahab's story is *big*. Even more exciting is this fact: Rahab's story is our story. But we still have a bit more ground to cover; let's see what happens next.

After consecrating the people and carrying out all of God's commands, Joshua launched a second attack on Ai. This time, the Israelites were successful. They burned the city to the ground and hanged the king on a tree before throwing his body at the city gate and covering it with a pile of stones. When all was finished, the city was left "a heap of ruins" (Josh. 8:28). That's a sober summary of events. But before embarking on the next conquest, Joshua wisely built an altar to the Lord and renewed the covenant by offering sacrifices to God and reading the words of God's law to all the people.

Read Joshua 8:30–35. What stands out to you the most in this passage?

Why?

My favorite part of the passage is the last verse: "There was not a word of all that Moses commanded that Joshua did not read before all the assembly of Israel, and the women, and the little ones, and the sojourners who lived among them."

The women. The sojourners. Everyone was included! Picture the scene as Rahab and her family come together with the rest of the community. Imagine them straining their necks to get a glimpse at the Ark of the Covenant of the Lord as rays of sunlight reflect off its gold carvings. Spreading a blanket in the warm desert sand, Rahab finds a place to sit with her family as Joshua begins reading. She leans forward, eager to drink in every word while marveling that the Creator of heaven and earth would save her and welcome her into His covenant family. She may not have understood everything that was spoken, but she understood enough.

Scripture teaches that when we are born again into God's family, we do not become a better version of our old selves. Rather, we are made completely new (2 Cor. 5:17). Once we were blind; now we can see (John 9:39; Eph. 1:18). Once we were separated from God and covered in sin; now we are cleansed and covered in the blood of Christ (Heb. 10:19–22). Once we were spiritually dead and deserving of hell (Eph. 2:1); now we are alive, and our citizenship is in heaven (Phil. 3:19–20).

While becoming a child of God happens the moment each of us repents and turns to Him, walking with God is also a daily task as we commit to learn His ways and follow in His footsteps.

.....................................YOUR TURN.....................................

Read Psalm 51:1-12 (optional: read the full psalm).

Spend some time meditating on the passage you just read, and ask yourself these questions:

Do I have any unconfessed sin in my heart?

Is there anything that is stealing the joy of my salvation?

Is there anything or anyone besides God that I am putting my trust in?

Write a prayer of confession as God leads you; end your prayer with a praise for His mercy and forgiveness, asking Him to restore to you the "joy of your salvation" (Ps. 51:12).

If you do not sense anything needs to be confessed at this time, write a prayer of gratitude. Consider asking God if there is someone He might want you to reach out to with a message or prayer of encouragement.

DAY FOUR
Embracing the Fear of the Lord

After Joshua defeated the city of Ai, he continued to lead the Israelites in their conquest for the Promised Land. In one battle after another, they defeated numerous kings and divided conquered lands for inheritances among the tribes of Israel. Years later, when Joshua's life was nearing its end, he would gather the people and leaders together, reminding them of God's many blessings and His faithfulness in fulfilling His promises (Josh. 24:2–13).

But Joshua wasn't finished. Just as the first chapter of Joshua includes the often-quoted text, "be strong and courageous," the last chapter of Joshua includes another well-known passage: "But as for me and my house, we will serve the LORD" (Josh. 24:15). I have the verse inscribed above the front door of my new home. However, just as the popular phrase "Be strong and courageous" (Josh. 1:6, 1:9) is often disconnected from surrounding context (where the Lord exhorted Joshua to be careful to know and follow God's law), the same is true for the popular passage in the last chapter.

Read Joshua 24:14–15. What was the first thing Joshua exhorted the people to do? Complete the first sentence based on the passage.

Now therefore ________________ *and serve him in sincerity and in faithfulness.*

Reflect on the exhortation in the above sentence. Based on your experience, how often, on average, would you estimate this general exhortation is preached among Christian churches in the Western world today? Underline your response in the following list. Next, consider your church over the past year or two. Place a circle around the response in the same list below that best reflects the teaching in your church.

Weekly

Monthly

Several times a year

Rarely

Never

Consider your responses to the last question. If your answers were Rarely or Never, what difference do you think it makes?

Let's refresh our memories by looking at some of the women we have been studying. Next to the names, describe what difference it made to themselves or others to have a healthy fear of the Lord.

Shiphrah and Puah (see Exodus 1:8–9, 15–17, 20–21)

Rahab (see Joshua 2:9–13, 6:25)

How about you? Whom do you know personally that you consider has a healthy fear of the Lord? What about them gives you this impression?

What difference do you think it makes in their lives or in those around them?

When people hear or think about "fear of the Lord," thoughts of God's wrath and judgment may be what first come to mind. However, Scripture has some things to say that just might surprise us. Let's look at a few verses from several other Old Testament books to see what we can learn.

In the table, I have listed various benefits of fearing the Lord. Match each one with its corresponding scripture reference by drawing a line between them. I completed one for you.

Reference	Benefits
2 Kings 17:39	Everlasting steadfast love of the Lord
Psalm 25:14	Your name is written in God's book
Psalm 33:18	(Fountain of) life
Psalm 103:17	Ministry multiplies
Proverbs 9:10	Receiving praise
Proverbs 14:27	Friendship (or secret counsel) with the Lord
Proverbs 31:30	Wisdom
Malachi 3:16–17	(Eye of the) Lord watches over you
Acts 9:31	Deliverance from all your enemies

Reread the list of benefits in the previous table (these are just a few!).

Which one do you need from the Lord right now?

Take a few moments to reflect on its corresponding verse in your Bible (consider reading the surrounding passage). What is God telling you?

A Friend of Sinners

Rahab had not been raised in a community of believers or worshiping the God of Israel. Yet, the stories of how the Lord saved His people from slavery and gave them victory over their enemies did not fall on deaf ears. Had someone told Rahab that God would one day call her into His covenant family and weave her into the ancestry of the Savior of the world, can you picture her laughing out loud? With her shameful past, surely she could never have imagined that God would choose someone like her.

PAUSE TO PONDER

Have you ever experienced a time when you felt that your past disqualified you from serving God in some way? Maybe you are wrestling with these thoughts right now. How can you be encouraged by Rahab's story? What truth from God's Word do you need to be reminded of today? Take a few moments to read and reflect on 1 Corinthians 1:26–31.

Rahab was a prostitute. I was a party girl. The Israelites worshiped demons.[11] If not having a shameful past is a requirement for being chosen by God, there would be no one left to choose. God is not ashamed of those He redeems. He loves to take the broken, the sinful, and the outcast and transform them into witnesses of His power and grace. How else will the world recognize His marvelous grace?

Reflect on the previous paragraph. Look up the word *grace* in a Bible dictionary (if using a standard dictionary, look for one that includes a theological definition of *grace*). Write the definition below.

Why is grace so important?

Why is grace important to you?

God is not ashamed of His redeemed. He loves to transform the broken, the sinful, and the outcast. How else will the world recognize His marvelous grace?

When I was an unbeliever, I was familiar with some of the more famous Bible stories, such as Noah and the flood, Moses leading the Israelites in the Exodus, or Abraham and Sarah receiving God's promise of a son. I also knew there was a man named Jesus who some claimed rose from the dead. None of these stories attracted me to God or the Bible.

While Scripture reminds us that no one can come to God unless He draws them in (John 6:44), sometimes I wonder what might have happened had someone taken the time to tell me about the unsung heroes of the Bible—heroes like Hagar, the runaway slave girl who gave God a name; or the demoniac who became the first Gentile evangelist;[12] or Tamar, who, disguised as a prostitute, conceived twin sons by her father-in-law and ended up in the ancestry of Christ. Or Rahab—a prostitute living in a wicked city who helped Israelite spies in their quest for the Promised Land. Maybe nothing would have happened. Maybe everything would have changed. All I know is that I can relate much easier to these kinds of stories. The stories are messy, the characters made mistakes, but in the end, God redeemed each one of them. There is something beautiful about seeing God at work in the messy stories.

In the New Testament, the theme continues. Jesus invited people just like Rahab to follow Him. He was often accused of shocking behavior, including breaking the law and even being demon possessed! Jesus Himself acknowledged what people were saying about Him: "Look at him! A glutton and a drunkard, a friend of tax collectors and sinners!" (Matt. 11:19).

A friend of sinners. What a beautiful title for the Savior of a fallen world.

....YOUR TURN...

All of us, at one time or another, are in need of a "friend of sinners." At other times, God is calling us to represent Him by being that friend to someone else. Take some time with God in prayer, and ask Him to bring to mind someone you know personally who might be encouraged by Rahab's story.

What one step will you take this week to reach out to that person, perhaps offering to share what you've learned about Rahab—and God—through this study?

Write a prayer of commitment below.

There is something beautiful about seeing God at work in the messy stories.

"Greater love has no one than this, that someone lay down his life for his friends." —John 15:13

Day Five
Grafted into God's Covenant Family

As significant as Rahab's story is in the book of Joshua, Rahab's name never surfaces again in the Old Testament. However, when we come to the New Testament, Rahab is mentioned in not one but three books! And the passages where her name appears are not mere mentions, but in every case, they carry great significance. Few women of the Old Testament can make such a claim. Not even Ruth or Esther, who each have an entire book named after them, hold such a privileged position in the New Testament writings. What is it about Rahab that sets her apart? Let's begin by exploring each of the three places where Rahab's name appears in the New Testament to see what we can discover.

Read the following verses in your Bible. Next to each reference, describe how Rahab is introduced in that passage. Be specific. (I completed the first one for you.)

Matthew 1:5—*Salmon the father of Boaz by Rahab*

Hebrews 11:31

James 2:24–25

Compare and contrast how Rahab is presented in the three sets of passages you just read. Consider the surrounding context. Why do you suppose the writers chose to introduce her differently? (Note: this question is intended for discussion purposes; as such, there are no right or wrong answers.)

Woven into the Lineage of Christ

Read Matthew 1:1–6. Based on the genealogy, write the name of each of Rahab's relatives. I completed one for you since we briefly covered it earlier.

Son:

Husband: *Salmon*

Father-in-law:

Next, read 1 Chronicles 2:10 and Numbers 2:3. How is Rahab's father-in-law described?

I find some of the details in God's Word to be fascinating. Even the genealogies can be rich with insights. As God works through the generations of His people, some of those whom He chose to weave into His redemptive plan can leave us shaking our heads (until we take a close look at our own lives and realize we are not much different).

Of the twelve sons of Jacob, God blessed the tribe of Judah with the honor of continuing the line leading to the birth of the Savior of the world. Tamar, Judah's Canaanite daughter-in-law who disguised herself as a prostitute, was the one chosen by God to bear the first son placed in Judah's royal line. If that union were not scandalous enough, only five generations later, we meet Rahab, a Canaanite prostitute whom God likewise blessed with the honor of being woven into the royal family line. The first two women listed in the lineage of Christ, and both had a past tainted by prostitution? Is this merely a coincidence? No. Nothing in Scripture is random.

Then we get an even more shocking picture: the husband God chose for Rahab was the son of Nahshon—"prince of the sons of Judah" (1 Chron. 2:10). The prostitute married a prince! This is the stuff of Hollywood movies and romance novels. The heartbeat of the Bible—God's passionate pursuit of His adulterous bride—echoes within the depths of every human heart. For Rahab the prostitute to become a bride fitting for a prince of Judah is truly a testament to her transformed life and God's astonishing grace.

This is one of the reasons why James and the writer of Hebrews chose to mention Rahab's old life—as a testimony to the power and grace of God. However, there is more to Rahab's story than meets the eye. Before we dive into the next New Testament passages where Rahab's name appears, we need to skip ahead in Matthew 1 to where the angel of the Lord spoke to Joseph, betrothed to Mary, in a dream.

Read Matthew 1:18–21. What reason did the angel give for the name chosen for the son Mary would bear, according to verse 21?

Rahab's privileged position in the New Testament writings is truly a testament to her transformed life and God's astonishing grace.

Fill in the blank to complete the meaning of the name *Joshua* from Week One. (Hint: see page 48.)

Yahweh (the Lord) ____________

During Jesus's lifetime on earth, the name Jesus (which is the Greek form of the Old Testament name Joshua) was quite common. Joshua was a hero to the Jewish people—and for good reason. He was faithful to God and was instrumental in carrying out God's promise to bring His people into the Promised Land. As such, the name Jesus (Joshua) was a popular choice among Jewish parents selecting names for their sons. The name was so common that in the Gospels and the book of Acts, Jesus is often referred to as Jesus of Nazareth. While at times this description was intended as an insult (John 1:45–46), it also was used to simply distinguish Him from others who had the same name.[13]

When Jesus was born, the Jewish people were eagerly waiting for their promised Messiah, whom they envisioned would immediately crush their oppressors, usher in God's kingdom, and rule the world as its everlasting King. What a testimony of God's grace that Rahab—the first convert in Joshua's conquest for the Promised Land—married a prince of Judah and is woven into the ancestry of her Savior.

Named in the Honor Roll of Faith

But God was not finished with this legendary prostitute turned proselyte. As if being an ancestor of the Messiah were not honor enough, God had much more to teach us about our courageous heroine.

At the end of Week Two, we briefly explored Hebrews 11, affectionately known as the "honor roll of faith." We discovered that two women are singled out by name. Of all the women throughout biblical history whom God could have chosen to call out by name in this "honor roll of faith," He chose only two, and one of these was the Canaanite prostitute Rahab. Even if Rahab's name only appeared here in the New Testament, she would still hold a very distinguished place in the Bible.

The letter to the Hebrews is believed to have been written to Jewish Christians in the early church (perhaps in Jerusalem). Two of the letter's key themes are to challenge persecuted believers to live by faith and, even more importantly, to illustrate the absolute supremacy and sufficiency of the person and work of Jesus Christ (chapters 1–10). Concerning Christ's supremacy, from the first chapter all the way until we reach chapter 11, the writer presents numerous Old Testament heroes and practices, all of which are compared to Jesus who surpasses them all. While a full exploration of the book of Hebrews is beyond the scope of this study, let's take a brief look at several highlights leading up to chapter 11.

> "She will bear a son, and you shall call his name Jesus, for he will save his people from their sins."
> —Matthew 1:21

Listed below are several titles and descriptions of Jesus, alongside a list of verses from each of the first ten chapters of Hebrews. Next to each scripture reference, write the letter that best matches one of the descriptions of Jesus. I completed two for you.

Verses in Hebrews	Titles/Descriptions of Jesus
_______ 1:1–2	A. Our great high priest
_______ 2:10 (also 5:9)	B. High priest of a new, better covenant
_______ 3:3	C. The Son of God
___I___ 4:8	D. A priest forever, after the order of Melchizedek
_______ 4:14; 5:5	E. A sacrifice once and for all
___H___ 6:13–15	F. Greater than Moses
_______ 7:16–17, 23–25	G. The founder of our salvation
_______ 8:6, 13	H. Fulfillment of God's promise to Abraham
_______ 9:12, 28; 10:12–14	I. Greater than Joshua

PAUSE TO PONDER

Of the descriptions and titles of Jesus you examined in the previous table, which one stirs your heart or captures your attention the most? Explain. Which one seems least relevant to you personally? Why?

Imagine that you are a Jewish Christian living in the first century. Which descriptions or titles of Jesus listed in the previous table might capture your attention the most?

Explain.

Compare and contrast the description or title of Jesus that stirs your heart personally with those that might have been most meaningful to the Jewish Christians in the first century. Are they the same or different? Why do you think that is?

Personally, there are several titles that stir my heart (such as Son of God and "sacrifice once and for all"), but it is also a wonderful exercise to imagine how some of these might have been especially meaningful to the Jewish Christians living in the first century to whom the letter was originally written. Reflecting on Jesus as being greater than Moses or greater than Joshua reminds us of the incredible foundation upon which our faith is anchored. Much of the New Testament would have little meaning without the Old Testament as its backdrop. The New Testament is filled with numerous direct and indirect references to the Old Testament, which would have been easily recognized by the Jewish people living in the first century.

In Hebrews 8:8–12 and again in 10:15–17, the writer pauses to quote from the Old Testament book of Jeremiah. Read Jeremiah 31:31–34. Why was a new covenant necessary, according to this passage?

> Much of the New Testament would have little meaning without the Old Testament as its backdrop.

Consider the description God uses of Himself in Jeremiah 31:32. What does this reveal about God's heart toward His people?

What was God's response to His people regarding the broken covenant? Circle one.

He abandoned them.

He punished them.

He forgave them.

God never changes. His love for us never changes. It is steadfast, infinite, and eternal. There is nothing you or I have ever done, or could ever do, that would change God's love for us.

························YOUR TURN·····························

When you do something that you know grieves God, what is your typical first reaction? What do you imagine God wants to do? Circle one.

Abandon you

Punish you

Forgive you

If you circled "abandon" or "punish," how might this further grieve God's heart?

Read Isaiah 54:5 in the margin. Take a few moments to reflect on God being a husband to His people and His willingness to even forgive the betrayal of His love. Write a prayer to God thanking Him for who He is.

Lesson Summary

What scripture, statement, or thought was most significant to you this week? Write it down, and then reword it into a prayer of response to God.

Notes

[1] The Greek verb form in this passage is perfect active indicative. The use of the indicative mood means that the author is making a statement of fact.

[2] Jerome F. D. Creach, "Joshua," in *Interpretation: A Bible Commentary for Teaching and Preaching* (Louisville, KY: Westminster John Knox Press, 2003), 68.

[3] Warren Austin Gage, *Gospel Typology in Joshua and Revelation* (Fort Lauderdale: St. Andrews House, 2013).

[4] Gage, *Gospel Typology in Joshua and Revelation*.

[5] Creach, "Joshua," 65.

[6] John H. Walton and J. Harvey Walton, *The Lost World of the Israelite Conquest: Covenant, Retribution, and the Fate of the Canaanites* (Downers Grove, IL: InterVarsity Press Academic: 2017), 256.

[7] Chet Roden, "Ai of Joshua," in *Lexham Bible Dictionary*, ed. John D. Barry et al. (Bellingham, WA: Lexham Press, 2016).

[8] Chris Hughes, *Rahab: Encountering the Woman Snatched from Destruction*, Face 2 Face series, ed. Simon J. Robinson (Leominster, UK: Day One, 2008), 65.

[9] Gage, *Gospel Typology in Joshua and Revelation*.

[10] Gage, *Gospel Typology in Joshua and Revelation*.

[11] See Numbers 25:2–3, Jeremiah 32:32–35, and 1 Corinthians 10:20.

[12] For a deeper exploration into this fascinating (and surprisingly beautiful) story of rescue and redemption, consider my Bible study, *Legion: Rediscovering the God Who Rescues Me* (Abilene, TX: Leafwood Publishers, 2019).

[13] Paul Douglas Gardner, *New International Encyclopedia of Bible Characters: The Complete Who's Who in the Bible* (Grand Rapids: Zondervan, 2001), 321.

NOTES

BELONGING TO THE GOD OF SALVATION

CAN YOU BELIEVE THIS IS OUR FINAL WEEK? TAKE A moment to appreciate how hard you have worked to reach this point. As much as I have loved all we have studied so far, I have been eager to begin this week's lesson. Rahab's story foreshadows events she could never have imagined—her story is also a foreshadow of our story. From the first page of Genesis to the last page of Revelation, from the first battle for the Promised Land to the final battle at Jerusalem, God is orchestrating His plan of salvation—to bring His beloved bride safely home.

Are you ready? Let's get started.

DAY ONE
Following the Footsteps of the Faithful

We finished last week's lesson by doing a brief survey of ten power-packed chapters in the book of Hebrews that outline Christ's absolute supremacy and sufficiency in accomplishing salvation for all who trust in Him. The writer of Hebrews then turns his attention to commending key figures from the Old Testament for their faith. Each of their stories in Hebrews 11:1–31 begins with the simple but profoundly significant phrase, "By faith," followed by their names and what they did. The writer begins with the story of Abel, whose God-honoring sacrifice cost him his life. The last example of faith God chooses to recount in detail is none other than Rahab's. The entire list is aimed at drawing our attention to Rahab. Let's take a closer look.

Listed below are various people we encountered during our study of the Israelites entering the Promised Land. Place a check mark next to the one you would most expect to be commended for their faith in Hebrews 11.

☐ Joshua

☐ The two Israelite spies

☐ Rahab

☐ The priests of Israel

☐ The army (fighting men) of Israel

Read Hebrews 11:30–31. In the same list above, place a circle around the one(s) commended for their faith.

Are you surprised? Confused? Encouraged? Explain.

An Interruption

In Week Two of this study, we talked about the fact that in the book of Joshua, Rahab's story in chapter 2 essentially interrupts the narrative regarding the conquest of the Promised Land, which began in Joshua 1 and picks up right where it left off in Joshua 3. By Rahab's story being positioned at the start of the conquest story, we are given a glimpse of its theological significance.

In the same way, Hebrews 11, the famous "honor roll of faith," begins with a list of Old Testament saints specifically commended for their faith. After Abel, we read of the faith of Enoch, Noah, Abraham and Sarah, Isaac, Jacob, Joseph, Moses—men and women held in high esteem among the Jews; but then the author breaks the pattern. Rather than mentioning a person or group of people, he refers only to an event: the collapse of Jericho's walls. To the readers, this event immediately brings to mind the anticipated champion of the Israelites—Joshua—who led them into the Promised Land. But the readers are in for a shock, for the name of their beloved leader Joshua is deliberately omitted. A Canaanite prostitute named Rahab stands in his place.[1] The writer now has his audience's full attention.

The list in Hebrews 11 is intentionally structured to draw our attention to Rahab.

Rahab is the pivot point of the entire "honor roll of faith" in Hebrews 11. Immediately after commending Rahab and detailing the specific actions for which she is remembered, the writer races through a handful of other names, acknowledging that he would be remiss to not at least mention them. But this is the writer's point—he has already described the example of faith he wants to highlight: Rahab's. This is why his next words are, "And what more shall I say?" (Heb. 11:32). One biblical scholar explains that the hero list of Hebrews "was carefully designed to culminate with [Rahab's] example."[2]

If you were the person writing a commendation of Rahab's faith, what reason might you have given? Complete the sentence based on your answer:

By faith Rahab the prostitute did not perish with those who were disobedient, because ____

____

Read Hebrews 11:31 and answer the questions.

What reason is given for Rahab's commendation?

What group of people is Rahab compared to? Circle one.

    Canaanites

    Those who were disobedient

    Israelites

    None of the above

Next, read Hebrews 3:16–18. Who are described as disobedient in this passage? Circle one.

    Canaanites

    Israelites

    Israelites' wilderness generation

    None of the above

PAUSE TO PONDER

How are faith and obedience (or unbelief and disobedience) connected in Hebrews 11:31 and 3:13–18? What personal application can you apply to your own life?

Read James 2:21–25. How does this passage shed further light on Rahab's commendation in Hebrews 11:31?

"…how shall we escape if we neglect such a great salvation?" —Hebrews 2:3

God knows our hearts. He saw Rahab's faith. She can serve as an example to follow because her choice to protect the Israelite spies—even at the risk of her own life—reveals that her confession of faith was not merely words, but faith in action. This is what the writer of Hebrews was getting at. The audience he was writing to was facing persecution, and the writer was exhorting them to follow Rahab's example of faith. Similar to their hero Moses, Rahab was not afraid of defying the king (Heb. 11:27).

Even more, Rahab is the only person in Hebrews 11 explicitly compared with those who were disobedient and is said to have not been destroyed (Heb. 11:31).[3] The writer highlights Rahab's example to draw a dramatic contrast. She is obviously contrasted against the citizens of Jericho (even though they are never specifically mentioned): Rahab was saved, unlike those who "were disobedient" (Heb. 11:31) and perished. However, earlier in his letter, the writer also spends quite some time warning his readers not to follow in the footsteps of the wilderness generation who perished because of their "disobedience" (Heb. 3:18 and 4:6). These are the only people specifically called out for their "disobedience."

This is what makes the list in Hebrews 11 so astonishing. Not only would the original readers of the letter have been surprised to see Rahab named instead of Joshua in the account of the fall of Jericho, but her faith—rather than Joshua's—is contrasted against the faithless (disobedient) Israelites in the wilderness the writer spoke of a few chapters earlier. To the readers, this would have been quite a plot twist. After all, when God first brought His people to the Promised Land, it was Joshua (and Caleb) who had faith! Not only that, but Joshua was a hero; he led the people into the Promised Land! And yet, after recounting the faithlessness and disobedience of the generation who refused to trust God and enter the land, the writer of Hebrews highlights the faith of Rahab—not Joshua—by saying, "By faith Rahab the prostitute did not perish with those who were disobedient . . ." (Heb. 11:31). By drawing a contrast between faithful Rahab and the unfaithful Israelites, the writer in effect elevates Rahab above Joshua![4]

The writer then encourages his audience—including us—to heed the example of Rahab and others:

> Therefore, since we are surrounded by so great a cloud of witnesses, let us also lay aside every weight, and sin which clings so closely, and let us run with endurance the race that is set before us, looking to Jesus, the founder and perfecter of our faith, who for the joy that was set before him endured the cross, despising the shame, and is seated at the right hand of the throne of God. (Heb. 12:1–2)

Since becoming a Christian, I have read this passage many times, often focusing on Jesus and the incredible price He paid for us. But every so often, I'll stop and reflect on the "great . . . cloud of witnesses" (Heb. 12:1)—trying to imagine Abraham and Sarah, Noah, or Moses cheering me on as I seek to live by faith. But I must confess, as many times as I have reflected on this "cloud of witnesses," in spite of the numerous times I have read the stories recounted in Hebrews 11, Rahab never entered my mind—not once. Now that I have spent the past year exploring her story, I believe that is about to change.

Outside the Camp

There is one last connection between Hebrews and the book of Joshua we will cover, a connection that I never noticed before writing this study, and it is one we do not want to miss!

In the Old Testament, God outlined numerous laws, regulations, and sacrifices for His people to follow. Concerning sacrifices for sin, the law required that the remains of the sacrifice were to be burned "outside the camp" (Exod. 29:14). References to this requirement can be found in Exodus, Leviticus, and Numbers (Exod. 29:14; Lev. 4:21, 9:8–11, 16:27; Num. 19:9). In addition, any person who was considered unclean (that is, someone who was diseased, who touched a dead body, or who suffered some other ailment as outlined in the law) was also placed "outside the camp" until he or she was deemed clean again (see Leviticus 13:46, Numbers 12:15, and Deuteronomy 23:10).

The phrase "outside the camp" occurs twenty-three times in the first five books of the Bible. After that, it appears again only three times in the entire Bible: once in Joshua 6 and twice in Hebrews 13.

Refresh your memory by reading Joshua 6:23. Who was placed outside the camp?

Although the reason is not explicitly stated, why might the leaders of the Israelites have placed them outside the camp?

Next, read Hebrews 13:11–13. What were believers exhorted to do, and why?

Compare this exhortation with Rahab's experience. What conclusions can you draw?

In the Bible, being sent "outside the camp" was to be excluded from the community because of being unclean. Regardless of the reason, the person would undoubtedly suffer shame. Sandwiched between the Old Testament Law (first five books) and the New Testament, there is only one incident of someone specifically being placed "outside the camp"—Rahab (along with her family). She and her family were placed outside the camp not because they were physically unclean, but because they were spiritually unclean due to their prior association with the wicked city of Jericho.

In this regard, Rahab was a foreshadow of the church. She bore the reproach outside the camp because she was willing to abandon the wicked city and cling to the one true God. In the same way, you and I are called to leave our old lives behind and "go to [Jesus] outside the camp and bear the reproach he endured" (Heb. 13:13).

Read Hebrews 13:14. How does this verse reflect Rahab's experience?

What would Rahab have to leave behind to become a member of God's covenant community? Circle all that apply.

> identity (citizenship) in a prosperous pagan city

> a familiar community (perhaps friends)

> pagan gods

> immediate family

> home and most (if not all) possessions

> her profession

Of the things you circled, which do you suppose might have been most difficult for Rahab to leave behind?

Explain.

Reflect on the audience to which the letter of Hebrews was originally written. What comfort would the words in verse 13:14 have had for persecuted believers living in Jerusalem in the first century? (Hint: see Mark 13:1–2 and Luke 19:41–44.)

Don't you love how all of Scripture is woven together? We can study and search its depths until the end of time and still feel as if we have only scratched the surface. Rahab's story is beautiful on so many levels, perhaps most especially because her story is a reflection of our own. Like Rahab, we are in desperate need of rescue. Apart from God's intervention, there is no way of escape. In love and mercy, He is drawn to every heart that responds to Him in faith. Once we belong to Him, we become part of God's covenant family forever.

YOUR TURN

Take a few moments to reflect on Hebrews 13:13–14. List four or five things you have left behind as a believer.

Of the list you made, which has been most difficult for you? Why?

Is there anything you are still holding on to that God may want you to leave behind?

What commitment will you make? Write a prayer as God leads you.

DAY TWO
Awaiting Our Heavenly Home

Years ago, I shared a home with two dear friends. Together, we decided to welcome a miniature schnauzer to the family; he was a sweet, gentle creature that we decided to name Mozart. Mozart and I loved going on neighborhood walks, and he especially looked forward to the nearby park where dogs were permitted to run without a leash. But freedom from the leash was not the only reason Mozart loved the park. Most of all, it was anticipation of the game.

And it never failed to disappoint. Mozart's nemesis was always there, ready and waiting. It took only moments before Mozart spotted it: a grey squirrel spread-eagle across the trunk of a tree, head jutted out, as if waiting for Mozart to notice. Mozart made a mad dash for the tree, determined to catch the instigating little squirrel. Just before Mozart made his final leap to reach the base of the tree, as if on cue, the squirrel scrambled back up the trunk, but not too far. Like Mozart, it appeared that squirrels enjoyed this familiar game of chase as well. By the looks of it, this was probably not the squirrel's first rodeo.

Mozart tried everything: scratching, barking, jumping. Over and over, the squirrel climbed down the tree just far enough to tease the dog, getting him to bark louder and jump higher, only to scramble back up the tree, never coming close enough to risk being caught. Amused, I watched Mozart—such torment! And yet, he kept on trying, refusing to abandon his hope of catching that squirrel.

Who could blame him? The world is filled with tempting delights promising to bring joy and fulfillment. Yet we know that had Mozart been successful, he'd quickly realize his prize was not all he had hoped. What would he do with the squirrel once he caught it? Even if Mozart had been the kind of dog who might have tried to eat the squirrel, I can just picture the squirrel scratching and biting at the poor dog's face until he was finally set free.

In some ways, many of us are just like Mozart. We chase the dreams, climb the corporate ladder, and exhaust ourselves trying in vain to grasp the next big prize, only for it to elude us every time. We can even overexert ourselves in ministry (Luke 10:38–42). But in the end, lasting joy escapes us. We are barking up the wrong tree. Jesus understood this when He reminded His followers, "seek first the kingdom of God and his righteousness, and all these things will be added to you" (Matt. 6:33).

Our Citizenship Is in Heaven

Read Hebrews 11:13–16 and 11:39. What promise were the Old Testament saints waiting for, according to Hebrews 11:14, 16?

Read Philippians 3:20–21. How does the New Testament continue this theme?

After recounting numerous heroes of the faith, the writer of Hebrews tells us, "And all these [faithful saints], though commended through their faith, did not receive what was promised" (Heb. 11:39). When we consider that God is faithful and good, it seems strange to read that those most commended for their faith "did not receive what was promised." Of course, there is more to the verse, and the story, but before we move forward, I would first like to ask you a question.

Think about the last time you eagerly waited for the arrival of a major event, such as a wedding, graduation, the birth of a child or grandchild, or moving into your first home. What was the event, and how long did you wait for it to arrive?

How did your thoughts, feelings, and actions change during your season of waiting? For example, did the event consume your thoughts? Did you prepare? Did you share your anticipation with others? Explain.

In Greek, the verb "await" in Philippians 3:20 is *apekdechometha*, which means to *eagerly* await. But let's be honest: it can be difficult to eagerly await Christ's return when our minds and hearts are occupied with other things. All too often, the joys and cares of this life push our hope of heaven into the background. However, when we make a diligent effort to "seek first the kingdom of God and His righteousness" (Matt. 6:33), all the other things in life will fall into proper perspective. Instead of chasing dreams, we meet the Dream Giver; instead of climbing the corporate ladder, we are promised to reign with Christ forever; instead of longing for the next big thing, we meet the Creator of all things. The world is bursting with trees filled with empty promises, but there is only one tree that truly delivers: the one fashioned into a cross.

With Possession Comes Responsibility

In Joshua's conquest for the Promised Land, the people of Israel experienced God's faithfulness in seeing the beginning of the fulfillment of God's promises: the Lord brought them into the land, He fought their battles, and territories were assigned to various tribes as an inheritance (Josh. 21:43–45). When Joshua was nearing the end of his life, he called together and spoke to Israel's leaders. He reminded them of God's faithfulness and warned them to continue to love and worship God since there was still more land to possess. However, with the possession of the land also came responsibility. Joshua knew the people would face many temptations and strictly warned them not to turn to other "gods." He warned them not once but six times![5]

It can be difficult to eagerly await Christ's return when our minds and hearts are occupied with other things.

"But seek first the kingdom of God and his righteousness, and all these things will be added to you."

—Matthew 6:33

Read Joshua 23:13. List every consequence that the Israelites would face if they disobeyed God by worshiping other gods and mixing with the people of the land. Be specific. I started the first and last ones for you.

1. God would no longer ____.

2. ____.

3. ____.

4. ____.

5. You will perish from ____.

Read Joshua 24:16–22. How did the people respond? What oath did they make?

Finally, skip ahead to the next book in the Bible and read Judges 2:1–5, 2:11–22, and 3:5–7 (optional: read all of 2:1–3:11).

Did the people fulfill their oath to the Lord? Explain.

Did the Lord fulfill His warning to the people? Explain. (Hint: glance back at Joshua 23:12–13.)

Look again at Judges 2:18–19. In your own words, describe the pattern of events identified in this passage.

How do you view God's handling of His people? Harsh? Merciful? Indifferent?

Explain.

Sadly, the events in Joshua and Judges (and all throughout the Bible) simply reflect the tragic fallout of the human condition. Adam and Eve wanted the forbidden fruit, Achan wanted the forbidden cloak, (Mozart wanted that feisty squirrel ☺), and the people of Israel chased after other gods (actually, demons; see 1 Corinthians 10:20).

You and I are no different. It is why these biblical stories are so vital to our learning. If God had not promised a Savior from the beginning (Gen. 3:15), we would have no hope of salvation. But praise God that there is hope! We have hope because God is faithful. He did send a Savior, just as He promised.

A Greater Rest to Come

Near the end of last week's lesson, you were asked which description of Jesus in the book of Hebrews stirs your heart or captures your attention the most. If I had to guess, the designation "Greater than Joshua" was not at the top of your list. However, a conquering Savior who defeats His enemies and ushers in a greater rest would have been of tremendous relevance to the Jewish people living in an enemy-occupied Promised Land in the first century.

Nevertheless, although God gave Joshua success in leading the people into the Promised Land, and Scripture records that "the land had rest from war" (Josh. 11:23), the rest was only temporary. There still remained much land to possess (Josh. 13:1). In the end, the Israelites failed to expel the people from the land (Judg. 1:27–2:3) and repeatedly fell into idolatry (Judg. 2:11–19). This is why the writer of Hebrews could say that Joshua did not bring true rest to the people (Heb. 4:8), but Jesus has done what Joshua could not do. When it comes to the fulfillment of all of God's promises, only Jesus can truly say, "It is finished" (John 19:30).

PAUSE TO PONDER

Look back at the table you completed on page 192 at the end of last week's lesson. List all the ways that you recognize Jesus as being greater than Joshua in a new light. Of the list you made, which stirs your heart the most? Why?

What's in a Name?

God could have chosen the name of any Old Testament saint to foreshadow the coming Savior of the world. We see glimpses of Christlikeness in the lives of Moses, Abraham, David, Boaz, and many others—yet God chose the name of none of these men; instead, He chose the name Joshua.

Ponder the meaning of the name Joshua, "The Lord saves," and the events we have been studying in the book of Joshua. What aspect of the story do you see reflected in his name? Circle one.

The Israelites were saved.

The citizens of Jericho were saved.

Joshua was saved.

Rahab and her family were saved.

The story is remarkable on many levels. To think that at the time of the Israelite conquest, the first person in the Promised Land to whom God revealed Himself as Savior was a Canaanite prostitute. Yet this serves as a beautiful reflection of God's character. We see it in the Old Testament as well as in the New Testament. The first person in the New Testament to whom Jesus revealed Himself as Messiah was a woman burdened with a shameful past. Though we are never told her name, she is famously known as "the woman at the well." We will take a brief look at her story tomorrow because it serves as a vital link between Rahab's story and key events in the book of Revelation, which I mentioned in Week Five. Stay tuned!

YOUR TURN

Earlier in today's lesson, you were asked to describe a time when you eagerly waited for the arrival of a major event (perhaps you are waiting for one right now). Reread Philippians 3:20-21. Compare and contrast your current eagerness

The first person living in the Promised Land to whom God revealed Himself as Savior was a Canaanite prostitute.

for Christ's return with the eagerness you had in anticipation of the event you described earlier. How is it similar? How is it different?

In the space below, write Philippians 3:20-21. Make it personal by replacing the plural pronouns with personal pronouns (use *my* instead of *our*, *I* instead of *we*).

____

____

____

____.

Read the words you just wrote two times out loud, and then spend some time with God in prayer. Record anything God is telling you.

DAY THREE
Tasting the Living Water

Today we begin our lesson with a brief look at the New Testament story of the Samaritan woman, otherwise known as "the woman at the well." The story includes the longest recorded conversation between Jesus and another person in the New Testament. Being a Samaritan, she was used to being looked down upon by the Jews.[6] Her reputation of immorality and the fact that she was a woman made it even more scandalous that Jesus would initiate a conversation with her.

Like Rahab, this woman knew the heartache of abandonment. After a string of broken relationships, perhaps she felt trapped in her circumstances but still dared to hold on to hope for the future. We can only wonder how many empty promises she had heard, how many unfulfilled dreams she had abandoned, until the day her Messiah came and asked her for a drink.

While we will not take a deep dive into her story, we will take a look at a few key elements, including one aspect of the story that appears just prior to the woman's encounter with Jesus at the well.

Read John 3:22–29. How did John the Baptist refer to Jesus?

In all four Gospels, this is the first and only direct reference to Jesus as bridegroom.[7] Because this is the only reference of its kind, where it is placed in Scripture is important. And guess what? This description of Jesus as bridegroom appears just prior to Jesus's encounter with the woman at the well.

Read John 4:1–26 and 4:39–42 to get an overview of the story. Why did the woman come to the well? What was she seeking? Circle one.

A husband

The Messiah

Conversation

Water

What was the first thing Jesus instructed the woman to do, according to verse 16?

Next, glance at verses 17–18 and 25–27.

How many husbands did the woman have in her past?

How many men was she in relationship with at that moment?

What was she waiting for?

"With joy you will draw water from the wells of salvation." —Isaiah 12:3

Finally, when the disciples arrived to witness the scene, what was their reaction? (Circle one.) The disciples

rebuked the woman.

questioned Jesus.

marveled at what they were seeing.

offered them both food.

Now for the fun part. Skip ahead in your Bible to the book of Revelation, which describes visions given to the apostle John. Read Revelation 17:1–6, and then answer the questions. What was the woman holding in her hand? (Circle one.)

Scepter

Cup

Weapon

Scarlet cord

When John witnessed the scene, what was his reaction? (Circle one.) He

fell facedown.

rebuked the woman.

questioned the angel.

marveled at what he was seeing.

There are several similarities between the woman in John 4 and the woman in Revelation 17: both were adulterers, both were on or near water, both possessed a drinking vessel, and in both scenes, those witnessing the events "marveled" (or were "amazed") (John 4:27; Rev. 17:6–7). At this point, you might be wondering, *This is all very interesting, but what happened to Rahab?* I can hardly wait for you to see how this all ties together. Hang tight—we're almost there!

The truth is that, apart from Christ, you and I are a lot like the Samaritan woman. We wander through life thirsty, filling our cup with the world's empty promises. But then God shows up and reveals another way. We have a choice to make: continue drinking from our cup of sin, or embrace Jesus's gift of living water. The only reason we can make this exchange is because Jesus took the cup you and I could never drink. "Are you able to drink the cup that I am to drink?" (Matt. 20:22), Jesus asked.[8]

PAUSE TO PONDER

Even if you have been a Christian for many years, where in your life right now are you trying to fill your cup with the world's empty promises?

What deeper heart desires may be at the root of your efforts? For example, are you looking for significance? Acceptance? Independence? Security? Something else?

What would it look like for you to surrender your desires to your heavenly Father, asking Him to fill your cup with true "living water" (John 7:37–38)?

Parallels in Revelation

If you ever are listening to someone preach or teach on Revelation, and the person announces that he or she has it all figured out . . . run!

This is perhaps one of the most memorable statements one of my seminary professors made regarding the book of Revelation. His words make me chuckle, and I still agree with his assessment. All throughout the New Testament, we are encouraged to anticipate the day when Jesus will return, cleanse the earth, set up His rightful kingdom, and make all things new. But before that happens, there will be a time in history unlike any other. These events are laid out in the book of Revelation.

For centuries, the book of Revelation has fascinated, baffled, and frustrated many students of the Bible. At this time in human history, our understanding of parts of the book are still speculation at best; even so, there are some things we can learn (2 Tim. 3:16). While a deep exploration into the book of Revelation is far beyond the scope of this study, today we will look at several parallels between Revelation and what we've been studying in the book of Joshua. While these parallels will not answer all our questions, they will provide a helpful framework for furthering our understanding as to why Rahab, especially her faith, is given such prominence in the New Testament.

Let's begin by reflecting on the events in Joshua when the Israelites prepared for their first battle to take the Promised Land.

Listed in the table are several events and concepts that appear in the book of Revelation. Place an X in the last column next to each event or concept if it also appears in the events we have been studying in the book of Joshua. I completed several for you. (Note: citing the Scripture references is optional.)

	Appears in Revelation	Appears in Joshua
A holy war was at hand	X 19:11–16	X 1:6, 2:24, 3:5–6, 5:15
The Ark of the Covenant appears in the narrative	X 11:19	
Two witnesses/men were sent into the city before the battle	X 11:1–13	
Divine commander/visitor appeared	X 1:9–16	
The commander/visitor had a sword	X 1:16	
The arrival of the commander caused the person to fall at his feet	X 1:17–18	
God's people (or churches) must be cleansed/prepared for holy war	X 1:11 (chapters 2–3)	X 5:2, 8–9, 15
The conquest involved seven trumpets	X chapters 8–11	
The conquest involved three series of sevens	X chapters 6, 8, 15, 16	
The people "fear God" (or were warned that they should) and know judgment is imminent	X 14:7	X 2:9–11
A great city was doomed to destruction	X 14:6–8	
A prostitute lived in (or was connected with) the great city	X 17:1, 18	
The prostitute was associated with the color scarlet	X 17:1–4	
God called His people (those who belonged to Him) out of the wicked city	X 18:4	X 6:17, 22–23
The city was burned with fire	X 18:18	
In the end, God's people received their inheritance	X 21:1–22:5	X chapters 14–19
Twelve stones (or precious stones) representing the twelve tribes of Israel were placed by the river	X 21:12, 19; 22:1–2	

Did anything in the table surprise you?

Explain.

The previous table lists just some of the highlights. One commentary author tells us,

> The Book of Joshua and its influence on Revelation has so far escaped the radar of modern scholarship, although it was widely recognized among the church fathers as a book prefiguring the end of the age. . . . They understood the profound significance of Joshua's battle against Jericho as a prefiguration of Jesus' battle against Jerusalem.[9]

Perhaps even more exciting (for the purpose of our study) is how Revelation will provide surprising insights into Rahab's story—as well as our own.

................................YOUR TURN................................

Before beginning this study, how significant would you have considered the book of Joshua for aiding your understanding of either the New Testament in general or the book of Revelation specifically? Place an X on the line to indicate your answer.

____

Not significant   Very significant

Explain your response.

In what ways, if any, have the past weeks of examining God's Word and Rahab's story impacted your

> view of Scripture in general?

> personal approach to studying God's Word?

> relationship with God personally?

DAY FOUR
The Whore Becomes a Bride

Yesterday, I enjoyed a fun visit with the women in my weekly Bible study group. Though the members in the group have changed over the years, we still call ourselves BSGE: Best Small Group Ever. During our casual conversation, a random question came up: "What is the strangest job you have ever had?" Joanne has a talent for doing voice impressions and shared that, when she worked at a department store, her coworkers urged her to make announcements over the store intercom using one of her many voices. Another shared how she worked at a restaurant that served Italian food on one side and Chinese food on the other. My friend Mary started working for the FBI when she was eighteen years old—and she's still there! When it was my turn, the only job that came to mind was the year I worked as a cocktail waitress at a nightclub. One woman asked, "Did you have to wear a skimpy outfit?"

The question caught me off guard. I had not thought about those days in a long time. I still remember the outfit: a small apron over a black pair of shorts and a T-shirt with the name of the nightclub. In truth, I didn't seek the job. I was dating one of the bartenders at the time and arrived at the club early while he was setting up. One of the waitresses failed to show up for work that night, and the owner asked if I would step in. Being in college at the time, the extra money was welcome.

After returning home from my Bible study group that night, I was lying in bed replaying the conversation in my mind. Reflecting on my days waitressing at the club, I was ashamed. Not so much for the outfit (it wasn't that bad), but for all the other mistakes I made during that season of drinking, drugs, and many other poor choices. Yet as soon as I was tempted to spiral into self-condemnation, three words burst into my thoughts: *she is dead*.

I held onto that thought and began repeating it, expanding upon it: *She is dead. I am not who I once was. I have been made new—not a better version of my old self, but an entirely new person. Jesus died to make me new.*

Scripture teaches that Jesus bore our shame on the cross (Heb. 12:2). Imagine how much it must grieve God when we allow previously confessed sin to shame us all over again, as if Christ died for nothing.

PAUSE TO PONDER

Is there something from your past that still haunts you today? If so, take a few moments to reread Hebrews 12:2, reminding yourself, perhaps even saying out loud: *I am not who I once was. I have been made new—not a better version of my old self, but an entirely new person. Jesus died to make me new.* Repeat it if you need to. Consider writing Hebrews 12:2 and 2 Corinthians 5:17 on a note card or in your journal and committing the verses to memory.

The reality is that all of us are in need of God's saving grace. Like Rahab, Tamar, and the Samaritan woman, all of us have a shameful past. As we have been studying these past weeks, we see that Israel had the same struggle. God repeatedly accused His people of being a faithless bride—even a prostitute (Isa. 1:21; Jer. 2–3; Mal. 2:11). We have not even looked at Ezekiel 16, where the word "whore" or "whoring" or adultery-themed wording occurs a whopping twenty-three times in twenty-four verses as God rebuked His people for forsaking Him. Or the book of Hosea, where God commanded the prophet Hosea—whose name is a variant of Joshua, by the way—to marry a prostitute to illustrate God's long-suffering faithfulness toward His beloved people Israel.

The theme continues into the New Testament, where Jesus is described as being the bridegroom of His church while James admonishes believers, calling them "You adulterous people!" (James 4:4). All of these converge into one overarching message of the Bible: like an unfaithful wife, we have prostituted ourselves, but God betroths us to Himself forever. We rebel, but God pursues us. We forsake Him, but He calls us back. In love, He redeems us, saves us, cleanses us, and transforms us into a pure and spotless bride.

The Kingdom of Heaven Is Near!

The message of salvation has never changed. Throughout Scripture, God's desire is for people to repent, to confess their sin and rebellion, and to turn to Him for salvation. Just as the people of Jericho fell into only one of two camps, so it has been from the beginning of human history and will continue until the end of time. Every human being must make a choice.

At the beginning of Jesus's ministry, He proclaimed one simple message: "Repent, for the kingdom of heaven is at hand" (Matt. 4:17). It is no coincidence that all four Gospels record that Jesus started His ministry in the identical region

"Return, faithless Israel ... for I am merciful ... I will not be angry forever. Only acknowledge your guilt, that you ... scattered your favors among foreigners ... Return, O faithless children, declares the Lord." —Jeremiah 3:12–14

where Joshua and the Israelites crossed the Jordan and stepped into the Promised Land,[10] which foreshadowed an even greater victory to come.

Read Revelation 14:6–7. What is the "eternal gospel" according to this passage?

Compare the angel's message with Rahab's confession of faith back in Joshua 2:9–11. How are they similar? How are they different?

Reflect on the message of salvation you might typically share with an unbeliever. Compare this with the "eternal gospel" in Revelation 14:7. How are they similar? How are they different?

Even at the end of time, as recounted in the book of Revelation, God is merciful, calling people to repentance. First, the call goes out to the churches (Rev. 2–3; see Revelation 3:19). From there, the message goes out to all the earth. Tragically, the majority of mankind "did not repent" (Rev. 9:20, 16:9, 16:11). In fact, they cursed God (Rev. 16:11).

SUPPLEMENTAL READING

WHO IS THE PROSTITUTE IN REVELATION?

Yesterday, we looked at a few passages regarding the prostitute in Revelation. But who or what is this prostitute? Many theories abound as to the identity of the prostitute in Revelation. We will not attempt to untangle them all; nevertheless, for the purposes of our study, there are some clues worth exploring.

Read the three verses printed below. Underline every description or clue concerning the identity of the prostitute. I completed the first one for you, revealing that the prostitute also represented "the great city" (Rev. 17:18).

And the woman that you saw is <u>the great city that has dominion over the kings of the earth</u>. —Revelation 17:18

> . . . and their dead bodies will lie in the street of the great city that
> symbolically is called Sodom and Egypt, where their Lord was crucified.
> —Revelation 11:8 (Hint: see also Isaiah 1:1, 1:10; Jeremiah 23:14.)

> The great city was split into three parts . . . and God remembered Babylon
> the great, to make her drain the cup of the wine of the fury of his wrath.
> —Revelation 16:19

In light of the words and phrases you underlined, which of the following best matches the possible identity of the woman, who also represented a great city? Circle one.

Rome

Babylon

Egypt

Jerusalem

The world

Sodom

Explain your answer.

Read Isaiah 1:1–4, 21. How did the prophet describe God's beloved city of Jerusalem, according to verse 21?

When the apostle John saw the vision of the woman in Revelation, he "marveled greatly" (Rev. 17:6). The Greek verb is *ethaumasa* and means "'to be astonished,' and it often expresses an attitude of criticism, doubt or even . . . rejection."[11] In other words, John was not amazed at the sight; he was offended. John's reaction would make no sense, however, if the great city were Rome or Babylon—known enemies to the Jewish people at that time. But if this great city *where the Lord was crucified* (Rev. 11:8) was God's beloved city of Jerusalem, now that would certainly explain John's reaction. It would also align with the Old Testament pattern of God calling out His people for their adultery—and God mercifully calling His beloved bride back to Himself.

"Come now, let us reason together, says the LORD: though your sins are like scarlet, they shall be as white as snow; though they are red like crimson, they shall become like wool." —Isaiah 1:18

Return to Me

Printed below are Revelation 17:1 and 17:3 and 21:9–10. Read 17:1 and 17:3 out loud. Do the same for 21:9–10. Compare and contrast the two passages. Underline each similarity, and circle each contrast between the passages.

Revelation 17:1, 3	Revelation 21:9–10
Then one of the seven angels who had the seven bowls came and said to me, "Come, I will show you the judgment of the great prostitute who is seated on many waters . . ." And he carried me away in the Spirit into a wilderness, and I saw a woman sitting on a scarlet beast that was full of blasphemous names.	Then came one of the seven angels who had the seven bowls . . . and spoke to me, saying, "Come, I will show you the Bride, the wife of the Lamb." And he carried me away in the Spirit to a great, high mountain, and showed me the holy city Jerusalem coming down out of heaven from God.

In Revelation 21:9–10, the bride is not described as the wife of the Son, or of the Christ, or of the Lord, but rather as the wife of the Lamb. Why do you suppose John linked the wife to the Lamb in this passage?

The parallel wording between the two passages in Revelation was intentional. John wanted his readers to recognize a connection between the judgment of the prostitute and the revealing of the bride (the holy city Jerusalem, which refers to the people in the city). To this day, it is Christ's sacrifice as the Lamb of God (John 1:29) that makes it possible for God's people, who rebel and forsake Him though He is a husband to them, to be transformed into a holy bride.

Read Revelation 18:1–5, which takes place as the great city faced God's judgment and ultimate destruction. Reflect on verse 4; what does this reveal about God's heart?

The Great Exchange

Scripture teaches that believers are the bride of Christ. In love, God made a covenant to betroth us to Him forever. Before God saved us, we were like Rahab: a prostitute living in a wicked city doomed to destruction. We were also like the Samaritan woman, drinking from a filthy cup full of immorality. As shocking as it might seem, we were like the whore in Revelation—wrapped in a scarlet robe of sin. Just as God saved the prostitute Rahab, in love, He saves us out of a wicked world doomed to destruction. In mercy, He drank the cup we could not drink by taking upon Himself the punishment for sin. In astonishing grace, He took the whore's scarlet robe upon Himself and, in exchange, clothed His beloved bride with bright, pure linen (Matt. 27:27–28; Rev. 19:6–9).

Read Revelation 19:6-9. What does the fine linen stand for?

Reread James 2:21-26, which we briefly touched on earlier. In addition to Abraham, the father of our faith, who is the one other person James commends as righteous (or justified) for their actions?

Reflect on James 2:26. Why is it important that faith be linked with action?

Rahab appears in just two chapters in the entire Old Testament, and yet, in the New Testament, in addition to being in the lineage of the Messiah, she is honored for her faith in Hebrews 11 and commended as righteous in James 2—even alongside Abraham!

Rahab's prominence in key faith passages in the New Testament holds her up as an example for us to follow; Rahab's faith not only saved her, but it transformed her. True faith leads to transformation, which leads to action. It is going to look different for each one of us. There will be times when we fail, yet praise God that our salvation does not depend on our faithfulness, but on His (2 Tim. 2:13). That's the beauty of the gospel. Let us strive to have the faith of Rahab, yet let us rejoice that in God's kingdom, even the prodigals are welcomed home with open arms.

"These are the ones coming out of the great tribulation. They have washed their robes and made them white in the blood of the Lamb."
—Revelation 7:14

In our English bibles, the words "righteous" and "justified" in the New Testament are both translated from the same Greek word, *dikaioō*.

As theologically significant as Rahab's story is, at the end of the day, the shocking beauty of Rahab's story is simply this: by faith, the renegade prostitute became a royal bride. And friend, here is the truth: Rahab's story is *our* story.

························YOUR TURN·······························

Titus 2:11–14 is printed below. Read the passage out loud and then answer the questions that follow.

> For the grace of God has appeared, bringing salvation for all people, training us to renounce ungodliness and worldly passions, and to live self-controlled, upright, and godly lives in the present age, waiting for our blessed hope, the appearing of the glory of our great God and Savior Jesus Christ, who gave himself for us to redeem us from all lawlessness and to purify for himself a people for his own possession who are zealous for good works.

What was God after based on the last part of the passage?

What is our part?

What are we waiting for?

What does this mean to you personally?

What one action step will you take from what you have learned today?

DAY FIVE
Leaving a Legacy of Faith

I was nearing my manuscript deadline and close to finishing writing this chapter when I received a phone call from my brother in New York.

For the past twenty-five years, while living in California, I would make a trip to visit my family in New York at least once, sometimes twice, every year. Sometimes I would go at Christmas, but more often I'd visit in the spring or summer when we could enjoy the outdoors: family barbecues, day trips, or simply visiting my mom and sitting outside in the sunshine overlooking the water that met the back of her property line. I've been witnessing to my family for over twenty-five years—as long as I've been saved—at times wondering if my witness was making any difference at all.

Over the past year, my mom's health had been declining. Her heart mostly. I was there last Christmas, then returned in the spring, and again this past summer, where I spent a week visiting Mom at a rehabilitation center while she gained enough strength to return home. That was just a few months ago. Since then, I met with Mom on video calls twice each week. Sometimes she seemed well; other times she was too tired to talk.

Then, just two weeks before Christmas, my family decided to plan a gathering during Christmas week. Both of Mom's great-nephews would be in town, and I was the only other family member out of state. My brother called, saying, "I know it's really short notice and you were just here several times, but if you can make it, we're having Christmas dinner at my house on the 28th."

I had already told Mom I was planning to return to New York for Mother's Day. Traveling to the East Coast in winter is challenging enough; Christmas week is even worse. Though I made it without hiccups the prior year, I've missed Christmas dinners before due to being stuck at an airport. It was risky, and the thought of visiting in the spring—Mom's favorite time of year—was far more appealing. I was also on deadline to finish writing this Bible study. On top of that, I had other commitments. In short, my freedom to take more time off had its limits.

I decided to keep my original plan and wait to visit Mom in the spring. (As it turned out, the airlines had a major meltdown during Christmas week, with hundreds of flights cancelled and thousands of people stranded.) On the day of the family dinner, they called me on video, explaining that they had just finished singing "Rudolph the Red-Nosed Reindeer," and they voted that it was my turn to choose a song. Being caught off guard and pressed to come up with a song, the first song that popped into my mind was "Silent Night." However, I quickly dismissed it. No one in my family was Christian, and besides, how could we follow "Rudolph" with "Silent Night" anyway? For some ridiculous reason, the only other song I could think of in that moment was "Grandma Got Run Over by a Reindeer." Really? That's the song I chose? I cannot describe to you how terribly disappointed I was in myself. At least I could have suggested singing "Happy Birthday" to Jesus, but it was too late. The moment was gone. We sang the song, finished the call, and my family enjoyed Christmas dinner. Later, I was told that Mom was in good spirits that day, even laughing and making jokes. Apart from our short call, I missed it.

Barely three weeks later, Mom fell, broke her shoulder, and landed back in the hospital. That was awful enough, but none of us were prepared for what happened next. She caught an infection the next day, and barely twenty-four hours later, she was placed on life support. I raced to get back to New York. I cried silently on the airplane, comforted only in the fact that dozens of close friends were praying along with me that God would allow me to arrive in time to share Christ with Mom one last time and to say goodbye (despite years of witnessing to her, I was never certain where she stood with the Lord).

When I arrived at the hospital, I sat next to Mom's bed, stroking her hair, reading Scripture to her—never knowing whether she could hear me, but pleading with God to enable her to hear my voice. Through tears, I spoke to her: "Run to Jesus. Run to the Father. He is waiting for you with open arms. He has loved you since before you were born." All the while, I held her hand, asking her to squeeze my fingers if she could hear me. No response.

I continued, "Jesus died for you, proving His love for you. If you had been the only person on the planet, He still would have come just for you." When I said those words, Mom turned her head toward me ever so slightly. Her eyes opened and she seemed to look at me, but it was so brief and she was blind in one eye—oh Lord, did she hear? Did she respond?

With my family together in the hospital room, I decided to play the song I wished we had sung together on our video call: "Silent Night." After that song, I played and sang along to "Hallelujah, What a Savior." Along with my stepdad who never left her side, I stayed in Mom's hospital room that night. Mom passed into eternity the next morning.

Several days after Mom passed and all the arrangements were made, I scheduled my return flight back to California. The night before my trip home, I kept sensing I needed to postpone my flight and stay in New York one more day. *Why?* Everything was ready. I was packed, I had my ticket, and my ride to the airport was arranged. But I couldn't shake the feeling that I needed to postpone my trip one day. That night at around 11 p.m., I cancelled my flight and bought a new ticket for two days later.

The next day, with nothing particular to do, I decided to look around Mom's art studio. I had previously found two of Mom's journals in her bedroom. Each contained only a few entries: some childhood memories of immigrating to the United States, a dream of seeing a chorus of angels singing, and even short letters to me, my brother, and my stepfather—which we each treasured. As I looked around the studio, there was a small bookshelf. Then I saw it: a journal I gave to my mom twenty years earlier. I remember when it happened. We had prayed together, and she asked Jesus to forgive her sins. The journal had just four entries. Part of one read:

> *Dear Father, please forgive my sins . . . help me to grow strong in my faith in you and your son Jesus Christ . . . Lord, thank you for my daughter, who has led me on the right path . . .*

I burst into tears and praised God! What a treasure! I had watched Mom struggle in her faith for more than two decades. At times, I saw brief signs of light—budding evidence of her faith, but because they were few, short-lived, and far between, I was never certain where she stood with God. It was God who kept me from leaving New York that day so that I would find this precious gift. Nevertheless, when I returned home to California, I began to doubt. *What if Mom didn't truly trust in Jesus? What if she wasn't entirely sincere? I never saw any real fruit.* That's when the Holy Spirit gently nudged me: Is it in God's nature to give someone false hope? Wasn't He the One who orchestrated events so that I could find Mom's journal in the first place?

Maybe I never saw spiritual fruit based on my expectations, but God knows her heart, and He alone knows how hard she must have fought to hold on to the faith she had. The Bible tells us that if anyone belongs to Him, "no one will snatch them out of my hand" (John 10:28). Although I was heartbroken to realize that I had missed the last family meal together with Mom, I can now rejoice in knowing that I will see her again—and when I do, we will enjoy a meal together unlike any other!

The Last Trumpet

Earlier in this study, we talked about the covenant Rahab made with the spies and the fact that the customary practice of sharing a meal together afterwards was missing from the story. The reason was simple: there was not enough time. But this omission foreshadows a greater meal yet to come. Long before Rahab spoke with the spies, God heard her heart. Long before Rahab made a covenant for her rescue, God made a covenant for her salvation—and ours (Eph. 1:4; Titus 1:2).

Scripture teaches that a day is coming when Jesus will sound the trumpet and gather to Himself all who are eagerly waiting for Him:

> For the Lord himself will descend from heaven with a cry of command, with the voice of an archangel, and with the sound of the trumpet of God. And the dead in Christ will rise first. Then we who are alive, who are left, will be caught up together with them in the clouds to meet the Lord in the air, and so we will always be with the Lord. Therefore encourage one another with these words. (1 Thess. 4:16–18)

Jesus is coming to fulfill God's covenant and claim His beloved bride. Like Rahab peering out her window, we know the time is imminent, but we do not know the exact day or hour. Yet unlike Rahab's earthly rescue, the covenant meal is not missing from our story. Scripture promises that a wedding feast awaits all who belong to Him! "Blessed are those who are invited to the marriage supper of the Lamb" (Rev. 19:9).

....YOUR TURN..

This side of heaven, you and I will never fully know the difference we are making in this world. We may never see spiritual fruit as we envision it should be, but God is always working, drawing hearts to Himself.

Today's lesson includes only one written assignment: *Leaving a Legacy of Faith*, which begins on the next page. I put this together to provide you with an opportunity to prayerfully reflect on the legacy you are leaving behind. Take the rest of the time you set aside for today's lesson and read the following instructions in preparation for writing your "Legacy of Faith."

Preparing to Write Your Legacy of Faith

Therefore let us go to [Jesus] outside the camp and
bear the reproach he endured. For here we have no lasting city,
but we seek the city that is to come.

Hebrews 13:13–14

Let us also follow in the footsteps of Rahab, who had a reverent fear of God. In faith, she hid the spies, gathered her family into her house, and waited for the last trumpet—the day of her salvation. Like the saints before and after her, she was looking forward to a heavenly home and a kingdom that cannot be shaken (Heb. 11:16, 12:28).

Instructions

Begin by examining your life since becoming a Christian. Reflect on all the ways God has enabled you to step out in faith for the advancement of His kingdom. This will look different for every person. You might want to reread the stories in Hebrews 11. As you do, be careful not to dismiss or minimize the path God has called you to as being less important. Each of us is responsible for the path God calls us to. He chooses our path, and all of us are called to make sacrifices. Notice that in Hebrews 11, no one is commended for the use of spiritual gifts, such as teaching or preaching or healing or giving. Rather, they are commended for their faith as revealed by their sacrifices and steps they took in light of their blessed hope for their heavenly home.

As you consider what your legacy might look like up to this point in your life, ask a few close friends or family members what sacrifices or steps of faith you have taken that stick out in their minds. If you keep journals, consider looking through them. To give you my own example, at this point in my life, I might begin my legacy statement with,

> *By faith, Shadia quit her full-time job and used her retirement funds to pay for seminary, not knowing what her future would hold. By faith, she has been witnessing to her family for over two decades, never knowing (until a few weeks ago!) whether it was making any difference for the kingdom of God. . . .*

Now it's your turn. When you finish, consider copying your statement into your journal, or use the elegant PDF version I created just for you, which you can download and print for free at www.shadiahrichi.com/rahab.

MY LEGACY OF FAITH

*And I am sure of this, that he who began a good work in you
will bring it to completion at the day of Jesus Christ.*

—Philippians 1:6

Date: _________

By faith,

Notes

[1] See Carl Mosser's careful study, "Rahab Outside the Camp," that documents her significant position in Hebrews 11 and the overall structure of the book in *The Epistle to the Hebrews and Christian Theology*, ed. Richard Bauckham et al. (Grand Rapids: Eerdmans, 2009), 394.

[2] Mosser, "Rahab Outside the Camp," 393.

[3] The point is not that Rahab was saved exclusively of all the others; rather, the writer is choosing Rahab's example in order to draw a specific contrast.

[4] Mosser, "Rahab Outside the Camp," 393.

[5] The six warning passages are found in Joshua 23:6–7, 12–13, 15–16; 24:14–15, 20, 23.

[6] Samaritans were a mix of both Jewish and Gentile descent and generally despised in the minds of pious Jews at that time. See John 4:9.

[7] Indirect references in the Gospels include Jesus relaying the parable of the ten virgins in Matthew 25 and Jesus responding to a question on fasting in three of the four Gospels.

[8] Although the passage continues by Jesus acknowledging that His disciples will also drink His "cup," here Jesus is referring to suffering for the gospel in general. But only Jesus could "drink the cup" of the cross, including the spiritual suffering.

[9] See Warren Austin Gage, *Gospel Typology in Joshua and Revelation* (Fort Lauderdale: St. Andrews House, 2013).

[10] See Matthew 3:13, Mark 1:9, Luke 3:3, and John 1:28.

[11] Georg Bertram, "Θαῦμα, Θαυμάζω, Θαυμάσιος, Θαυμαστός," in *Theological Dictionary of the New Testament*, ed. Gerhard Kittel, Geoffrey W. Bromiley, and Gerhard Friedrich (Grand Rapids: Eerdmans, 1965), 3:28.

Don't miss the first study in the Behind the Seen series!

HAGAR

Rediscovering the God Who Sees Me

Shadia Hrichi

ISBN 978-0-89112-470-2

Witness the depths of God's compassion through the eyes of a runaway slave.
How much do we really know about the young slave girl Hagar? She is often relegated to the backstage as a minor character in God's redemptive story. But was she? Do you know how her story ends? Rest assured that it does not end in despair. In fact, she emerges victorious! Through this seven-week, in-depth Bible study, you will find that when you surrender your life into God's hands, your trials and triumphs serve a magnificent purpose: to draw you into the arms of the faithful *God Who Sees Me.*

"Deep and packed with surprising insights! I enjoyed exploring the story of Hagar—an often-discarded woman who played a profound part in human history. . . . This study beautifully captures the depth of God's love for all people. I am excited to share it with others!"

> —**Francine Rivers,** international best-selling author

"This study is a personal and compelling guide to a powerful and under-appreciated story of God's faithfulness."

> —***Bible Study Magazine,*** a publication of Faithlife, the creator of Logos Bible Software

Visit shadiahrichi.com for updates on new books and resources in the Behind the Seen series.

The second study in the Behind the Seen series!

LEGION

Rediscovering the God Who Rescues Me

Shadia Hrichi

ISBN 978-1-68426-370-7

Tormented, chained, and living in a graveyard, the man known only by the name of the demons that tormented him had no one to help him—no one to intercede for him. No one but Jesus. Climb into the boat with Jesus as He heads into enemy territory. Witness Jesus's power and passion as He battles violent storms and armies of demons to rescue . . . one . . . lost . . . soul.

Through this six-week, action-packed study, you will experience God's relentless love as you celebrate the impassioned Savior Who moved heaven and earth to rescue you.

"Shadia has written another outstanding study. *Legion* is rich and in-depth. There were so many new insights; several brought tears to my eyes. Well written and well organized, this study is packed with valuable life lessons. I can't wait to read the next one!"

—**Francine Rivers,** international best-selling author

"Though one of the more obscure individuals to experience Christ's powerful rescuing love, this man's life is destined to become a much loved Bible story as Shadia leads you into his broken world. I highly recommend this stunning, thorough, unforgettable, hope-filled Bible study."

—**Dr. Phyllis Bennett,** director of the Women's Center for Ministry at Western Seminary

Visit shadiahrichi.com for updates on new books and resources in the Behind the Seen series.

Check out the third in Shadia's series!

TAMAR

Rediscovering the God Who Redeems Me

Shadia Hrichi

ISBN 978-1-68426-301-1

Nothing can thwart God's plan for your life—*not even you*. If God can choose the Canaanite Tamar to continue the line through which Christ would come, can anything keep Him from weaving your story into His redemptive plan?

Tamar, daughter-in-law of Judah, is the first woman listed in the lineage of Christ. Mistreated, widowed twice, betrayed, and used as a prostitute . . . it seems impossible that God could redeem her story, but His plan of redemption was prewritten for all eternity—and nothing can get in His way.

Through this six-week, in-depth Bible study, you will discover that no matter life's twists and turns or your sins and failures, there is a God working *behind the seen*, redeeming it all for His glory.

"If you enjoy squeezing every delicious drop of truth from the stories found in Scripture, Shadia Hrichi's new study on Tamar will delight you. She handles God's Word with exceeding care, pointing us to the many vital lessons worth learning and applying to our own lives."

—**Liz Curtis-Higgs,** best-selling author of *Bad Girls of the Bible*

"If you embark on a Shadia Hrichi Bible study, know that you are in good hands. Tamar's life altered the trajectory of human history, and this very engaging study will put those pieces together for you in this powerful picture of God at work in the midst of a mess. Highly recommended."

—**Susy Flory,** *New York Times* best-selling author and coauthor, and director of West Coast Christian Writers

Visit shadiahrichi.com for updates on new books and resources in the Behind the Seen series.